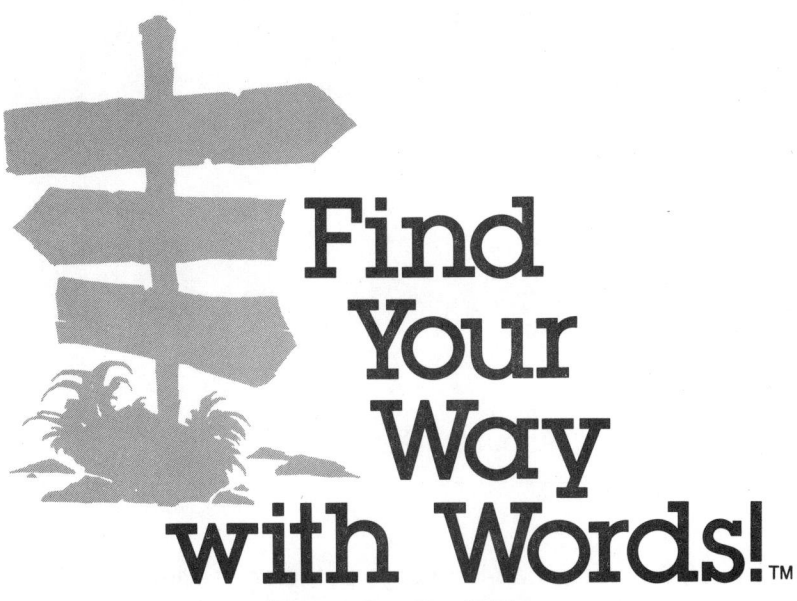

Find Your Way with Words!™

Fun Activities for Clear Communication

Jan Danielson

LinguiSystems, Inc.
3100 4th Avenue
East Moline, IL 61244

Problem / Skill Area: Vocabulary
Developmental Age: 7 thru 12 years
Interest Level: 2nd thru 6th grade

Copyright © 1987 LinguiSystems, Inc.

Limited Reproduction Allowed

LinguiSystems grants to individual teachers and other professionals the limited right to reproduce and distribute copies of these worksheets for non-commercial, face-to-face individual, group or classroom instruction. All copies must include LinguiSystems' copyright notice.

Reproduction and distribution of these worksheets for an entire school, school system or group of professionals is strictly prohibited.

1-800-PRO IDEA

ISBN 1-55999-038-4

About the Author

Jan Danielson, M.S., CCC is a speech-language pathologist with R.I.S.E. Special Services in Indianapolis, Indiana. She has worked extensively with speech and language-disordered students in the public school. **Find Your Way with Words** is her second publication with LinguiSystems. She is also author of **Vocabulary To Go** and **Writing To Go** and co-author of **More Vocabulary To Go**.

March 1990

Acknowledgments

I would like to express my appreciation to Christina Hill, art teacher, whose assistance and encouragement helped me develop an idea into a reality. Additional thanks go to Kathy Petrovic and Debbie Smanda, whose enthusiasm and feedback helped me to complete this work.

A final thank-you is reserved for my husband, Gerry, and my children, without whose patience and encouragement I could not have completed this manuscript.

Dedication

To my children, Claire, Andrew, and Laura

We welcome your comments on *Find Your Way With Words* and other LinguiSystems products. Please send your comments to:

Carolyn Blagden
Editorial Manager
LinguiSystems, Inc.
3100 4th Avenue
East Moline, IL 61244

Table of Contents

Introduction 5

Assessing 7
    Skills Checklist 8
    Sample Pictures 9

Teaching
    Lines, Shapes, and Designs 13
    Mazes, Maps, and Graphs 31
    Cut and Place 45
    Scene Descriptions 53
    Comparing through Similes 65
    Focusing on Important Features 73
    General Barrier Activities
        Level One 89
        Level Two 102
        Level Three 111
    Focusing on Discriminating Features 119
    Exclusion 131

Additional Suggestions 137

References 139

Introduction

Many language-impaired students who have mastered basic syntactic rules may still be ineffective communicators because of deficits in pragmatic, or functional, language skills. These students overuse nondescriptive words like "stuff" and "thing." They often supplement their language with gestures to clarify what they want to say. Their listeners are typically confused and in need of some clarification. For example, consider this verbatim description of a picture of a dog by a language-impaired ten year old girl: "It got little dots up here and some down there and a tail like an ocean thing with half dots and its tongue licking out."

Lloyd and Beveridge (1981) have summarized characteristics of poor communicators during referential communication tasks. Instead of focusing on critical attributes, poor speakers give irrelevant attributes, frequently demonstrating a bias toward one attribute, such as color. When they do give critical attributes, these attributes are often lost within a "rambling message." These speakers also use vague referents and fail to modify their descriptions in response to the listener's comments.

One effective way to bring inadequate or confusing language to the student's attention is to use barrier games or activities. Very simply, a barrier is placed between the listener and the speaker so that their view of each other is blocked. They are given identical pictures or objects. The listener selects the appropriate item on his side from the description the speaker provides. There are slight variations of this technique, but the objective is the same. To make the correct choice, the listener must have appropriate listening skills while the speaker must use specific descriptive language. Only then does effective verbal communication occur. The result of ineffective language is immediately apparent to the speaker due to the listener's failure to comply as directed. Conversely, effective language is immediately reinforced by the listener's success.

While barrier games have long been used as a therapy technique, little has been written about the cluster of skills needed to communicate effectively in barrier exercises. *Find Your Way with Words* is a resource of activities for remediating specific referential communication skills. Some language-impaired students seem to be especially weak in both giving and requesting information. Both these language functions are necessary to cope with the language demands of the classroom (Staab, 1986). Because barrier activities involve both listening and speaking roles, *Find Your Way with Words* provides meaningful, goal-oriented activities for acquiring these essential language skills.

General Instructions

Use the assessment procedure, page 7, to establish a baseline of referential communication skills. After identifying the areas of weakness in the student's language, proceed with the appropriate teaching worksheets. Then, reinforce the worksheet learning with the barrier activities. To expand upon these essential communication skills, refer to the additional suggested activities at the end of the manual.

The worksheets are arranged in order of difficulty. Some students may not be able to do all the worksheets in one unit. For these students, use only the easier worksheets from each unit that are appropriate to their areas of language difficulty.

After the student has completed *Find Your Way with Words,* re-evaluate his language skills with either the same or novel pictures. Comparison of the checklists between the two evaluations should reveal significant improvement in the student's referential communication skills.

Any manageable size group can participate in the barrier activities. If only one student is involved, participate with the student, alternating speaker and listener roles as appropriate. With groups of two or more, once the students have learned the task, have the students take turns playing the speaker and listener roles.

Find Your Way with Words need not be restricted to use with language-impaired students. The barrier activities are an excellent method for establishing carryover in articulation, fluency and voice disorders. *Find Your Way with Words* can also be used as supplementary language material in the classroom to improve language and cognitive skills.

Assessing

A student's description of sample pictures offers the instructor the opportunity to record how effectively he uses language to convey information. The instructor can observe what kind of organization, if any, the student uses in describing the pictures. Does the student begin with the topic and then proceed to the details, or does he name items randomly as he notices them? How appropriately does the student use directional terminology (*right, left, middle,* etc.)? When a student encounters a picture he does not recognize, does he attempt to describe it, or does he use nondescriptive words, like *thing* and *stuff?* Does the student gesture frequently to convey meaning, rather than using words? Most language-impaired students' performances will be indicated in the unshaded boxes of the checklist, demonstrating ineffective referential communication skills.

Instructions

It is best to tape-record the student's description of a sample scene, then transcribe it at the bottom of the checklist. However, because many language-impaired students tend to give simple, terse descriptions, it may be possible to transcribe as the student is speaking. Note specific behaviors as well as general impressions. For instance, latency in response can be recorded as "pause," and word retrieval difficulty indicated by "uh, uh, uh." Also, identify any pragmatic behaviors, such as the student's attempts to repair his ineffective statements.

To be sure the student's language difficulty is consistent across different levels of visual stimuli, give him several sample pictures to describe. Once the student has completed *Find Your Way with Words,* present the sample pictures or any appropriate novel pictures to the student as a postcheck. The general observations of the student's language skills should have shifted from the unshaded to the shaded boxes on the Skills Checklist, indicating improved referential communication skills.

Skills Checklist

Name _____   Date _____

Instruct the student to describe each scene so it could be drawn by a listener. Record the student's description and transcribe it verbatim at the bottom of this sheet. Present as many sample pictures as appropriate. After analyzing the transcriptions, check to what extent the following communication behaviors are present or absent.

Does the student _____?

	usually	sometimes	rarely
1. identify the kind of scene (farm, beach, etc.)	▓		
2. use "left-right" terminology	▓		
3. use directional words (*top, bottom, behind, middle,* etc.)	▓		
4. use size words appropriately	▓		
5. use similes (*looks like . . .*)	▓		
6. use descriptive words	▓		
7. go from general to more specific characteristics	▓		
8. give enough information to reconstruct the scene	▓		
9. overuse nondescriptive words			▓
10. depend on gestures for clarification			▓
11. coin a new word instead of using a correct word			▓
12. focus on or include unimportant details			▓

Transcription

_____

_____

_____

_____

Sample Picture A

Sample Picture B

Sample Picture C

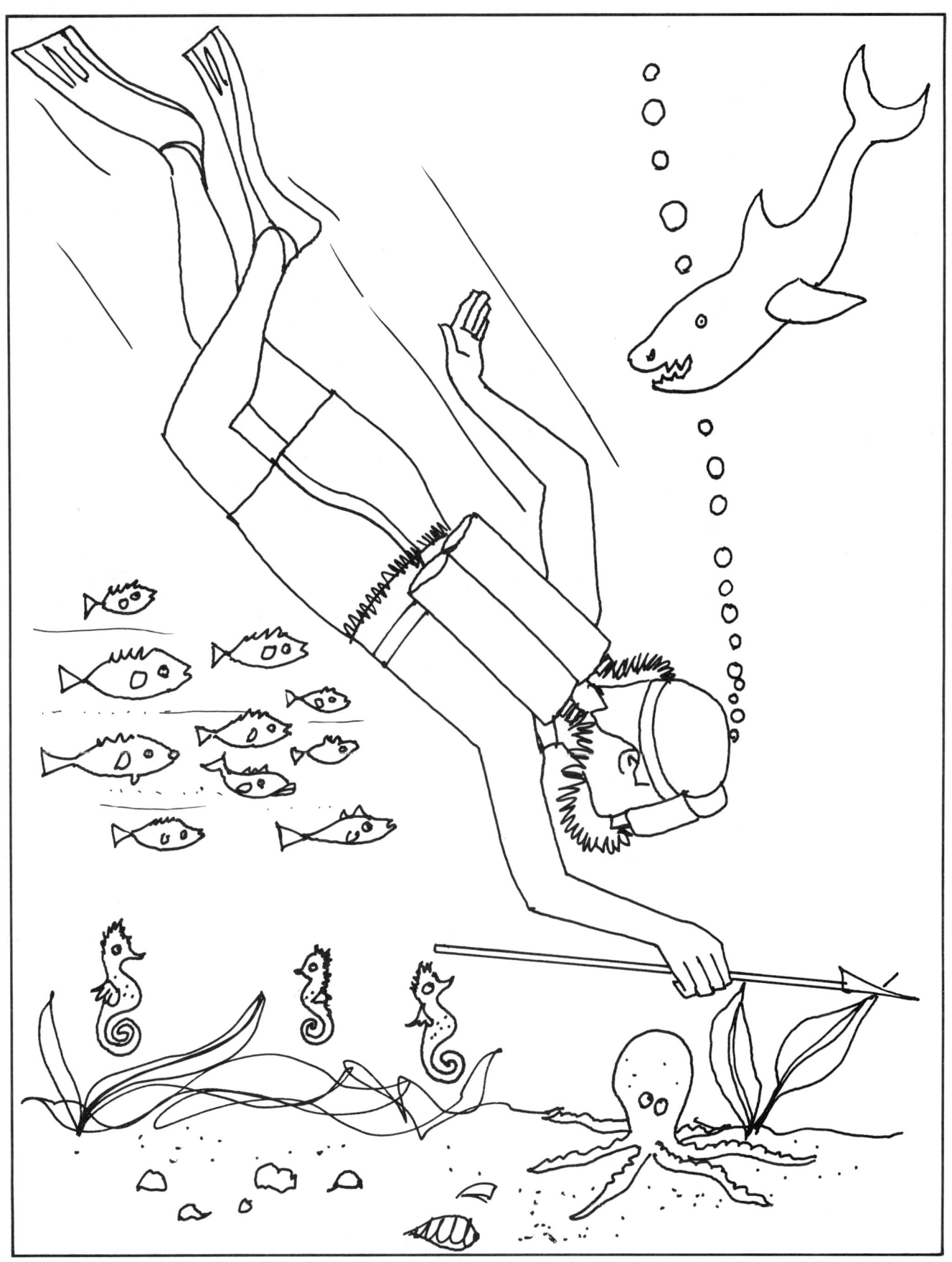

Sample Picture D

Lines, Shapes and Designs

Students are introduced to position and location concepts very early in life. They are instructed to place objects *on top of, behind,* and *under* other objects. Even before mastering the terms *left* and *right,* students learn the left shoe must go on the left foot. When students enter school, they learn left to right progression when reading and writing and they learn *top, bottom,* and *middle* concepts as necessary readiness skills. Yet, some students have difficulty mastering directional terms. *Left* and *right* terminology as well as shape terminology continue to be confused. Without a strong foundation in directional concepts, these students have difficulty with terms such as *horizontal, diagonal,* and *vertical.* Yet, they will be expected to use many of these concepts throughout their school experiences.

This unit reinforces these frequently needed shape and directional concepts. The student is guided through progressively more difficult tasks by gradually fading out written and verbal cues. For example, the student initially matches designs to their written descriptions. Later, the student generates the descriptive language necessary.

Instructions

Proceed through the worksheets of this unit in order. Hand out the first worksheet. Read, or have the student read, the instructions on each worksheet and fill out the worksheet accordingly. Each of these worksheets can be done as an oral or a written task.

Whenever appropriate, let the student use Direction Reminder A, page 14, or Direction Reminder B, page 15, as a guide to the correct terms to use.

The barrier activities reinforce the line, shape, and design concepts learned in the worksheets from this unit. The activities are arranged from easy to hard. For the students who are unable to complete the activities in this unit, proceed to the easier activities at the beginning of the next unit after reaching their competency level in this unit.

Choose one of the barrier activities on pages 28 through 30. Place a barrier between the students.

Step 1: Give each student a copy of the activity sheet. Describe one of the patterns for the students to circle.

Step 2: Give each student a copy of the activity sheet. Designate one of the students as the speaker. Have him describe a pattern for the others to identify.

Step 3: Give the speaker a copy of the activity sheet. Have him describe one of the patterns for the others to draw on a blank piece of paper.

Step 4: Have the students draw their own patterns. Then, have them take turns describing their original pattern for the others to draw.

Core Vocabulary

arc	line
beside	oval
block	rectangle
bottom	right
circle	S-curve
crescent	shape
cube	spiral
cylinder	square
design	straight
diagonal	stripe
diamond	top
dot	triangle
dotted	tube
down	up
half circle	upside-down
horizontal	vertical
inside	wavy
left	zigzag

Direction Reminder A

Name _____

Use this page to help you remember which way is *up, down, left,* and *right.*

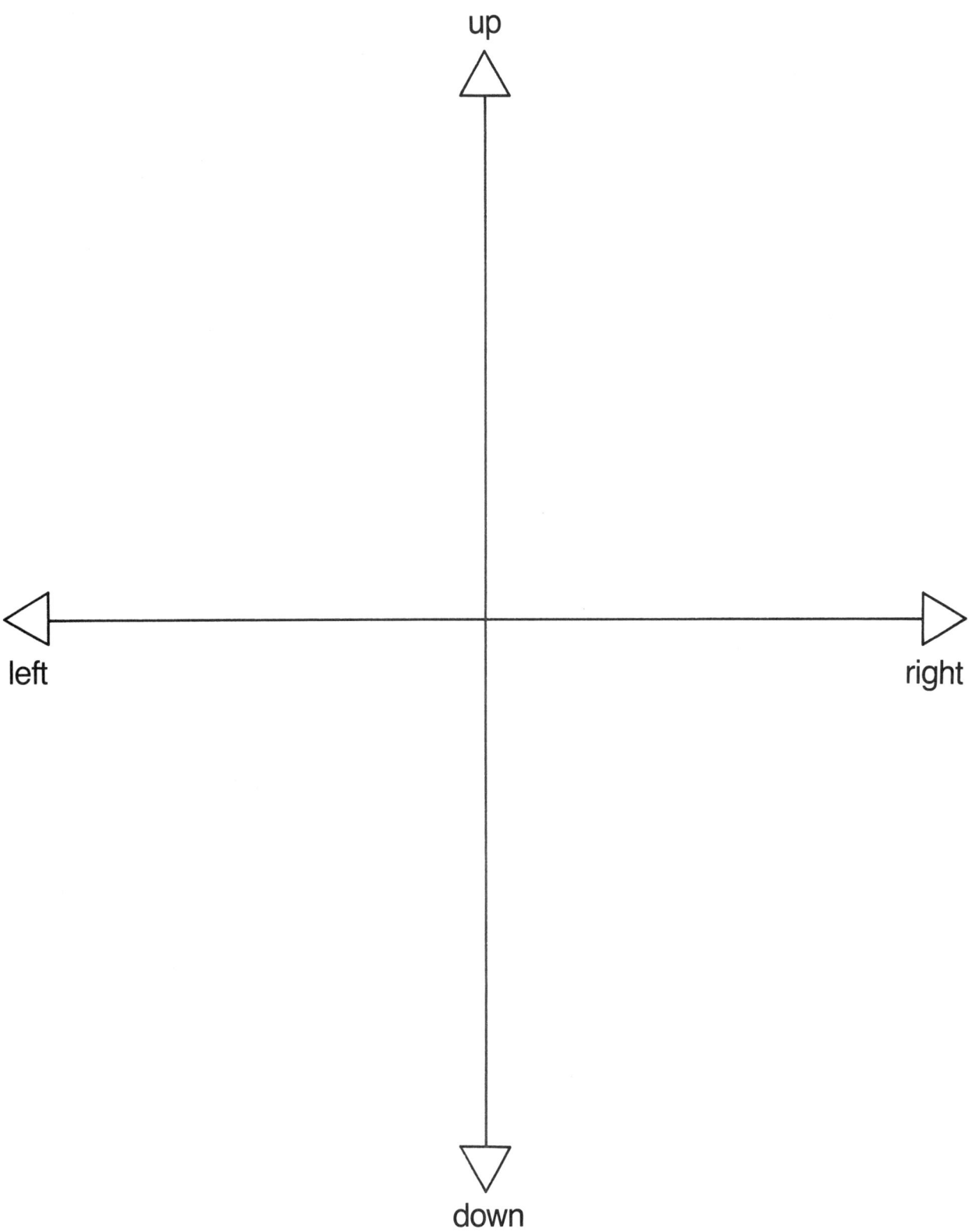

LINES, SHAPES, AND DESIGNS

Direction Reminder B

Name _____

Use this page to help you remember which way is *horizontal, vertical,* and *diagonal.*

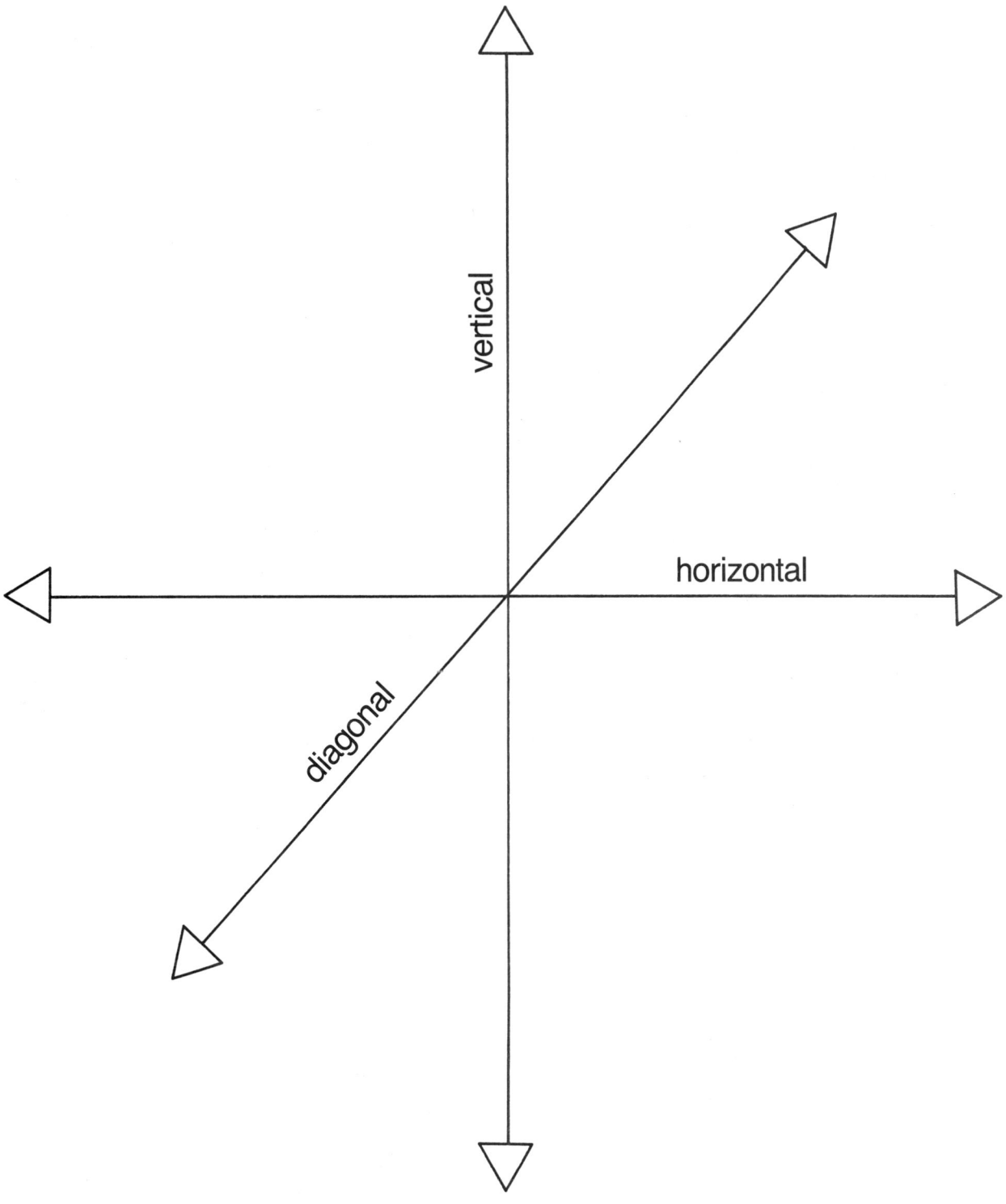

LINES, SHAPES, AND DESIGNS

Can You Match These Lines?   Name _____

Look at the lines below. Then, read the descriptions on the right. Match each line to its description by writing the correct letters in the blanks beside the lines.

_____ 1.   – – – – – – – – –

A. horizontal line

B. vertical line

C. diagonal line

D. dotted line

E. wavy line

_____ 2.   _____

_____ 3.

_____ 4.   /

_____ 5. |

LINES, SHAPES, AND DESIGNS

More Lines to Match   Name _____

Look at the lines below. Then, read the descriptions on the right. Match each line to its description by writing the correct letters in the blanks beside the lines.

_____ 1.

                                                  A. S-curve

                                                  B. spiral

                                                  C. arc

                                                  D. dot

                                                  E. zigzag

_____ 2.

_____ 3.

_____ 4.

_____ 5.

LINES, SHAPES, AND DESIGNS

What's My Line?

Name _____

Look at the lines below. Describe the lines in the blanks on the right. The first one is done for you.

1. _These are diagonal lines._ _____

2. _____

3. _____

4. _____

5. _____

LINES, SHAPES, AND DESIGNS

What About These Lines?

Name _____

Look at the lines below. Describe the lines in the blanks on the right.

1.
_____
_____
_____

2.
_____
_____
_____

3.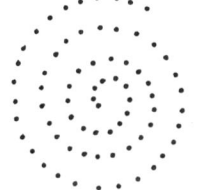
_____
_____
_____

4.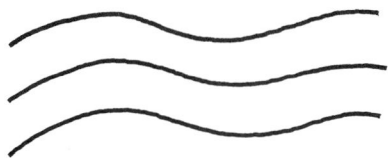
_____
_____
_____

5.
_____
_____
_____

LINES, SHAPES, AND DESIGNS

Can You Match These Shapes?

Name _____

Look at the shapes below. Then, read the descriptions on the right. Match each shape to its description by writing the correct letters in the blanks beside the shapes.

_____ 1.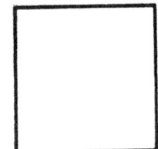

A. circle
B. triangle
C. rectangle
D. diamond
E. square

_____ 2.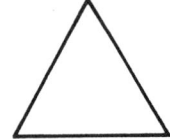

_____ 3.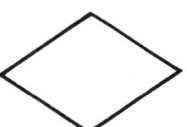

_____ 4.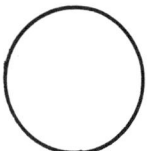

_____ 5.

LINES, SHAPES, AND DESIGNS

More Shapes to Match

Name _____

Look at the shapes below. Then, read the descriptions on the right. Match each shape to its description by writing the correct letters in the blanks beside the shapes.

_____ 1.

A. oval

B. tube or cylinder

C. half circle

D. block or cube

E. crescent

_____ 2.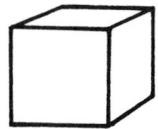

_____ 3.

_____ 4.

_____ 5.

LINES, SHAPES, AND DESIGNS   Copyright © 1987 LinguiSystems, Inc.

What's My Shape?   Name _____

Look at the shapes below. Describe the shapes in the blanks on the right. The first one is done for you.

1. 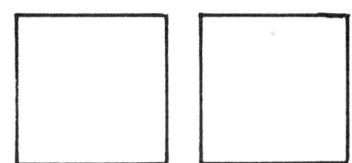 These are two squares beside each other.

2.  _____

3. 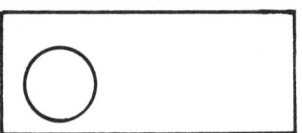 _____

4.  _____

5. 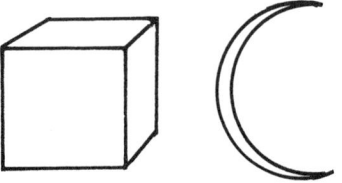 _____

LINES, SHAPES, AND DESIGNS

How About These Shapes?   Name _____

Look at the shapes below.   Describe the shapes in the blanks on the right.

1.

2.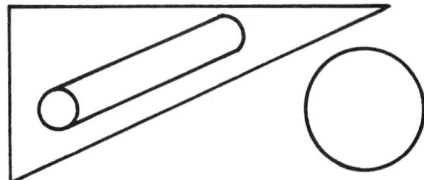

3.

4.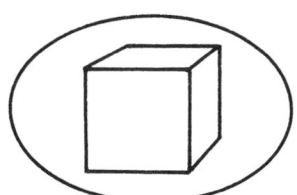

5.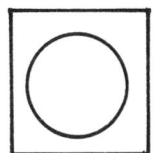

LINES, SHAPES, AND DESIGNS   Copyright © 1987 LinguiSystems, Inc.

Can You Match These Designs?

Name _____

Look at the designs below. Then, read the descriptions on the right. Match each design to its description by writing the correct letters in the blanks beside the designs.

_____ 1.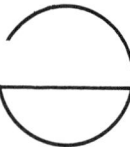

A. vertical straight line with a circle beside it at the top left side

B. half a circle

C. vertical straight line with a circle beside it at the bottom on the right side

_____ 2.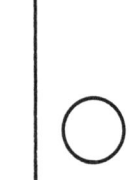

D. upside-down e-shape

E. half an oval

F. diagonal straight line with a circle beside it at the bottom on the right side

_____ 3.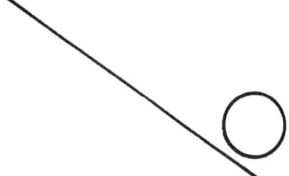

G. diagonal straight line

_____ 4.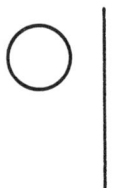

_____ 5.

LINES, SHAPES, AND DESIGNS

More Designs to Match

Name _____

Look at the designs below. Then, read the descriptions on the right. Match each design to its description by writing the correct letters in the blanks beside the designs.

_____ 1.

A. triangle inside a square
B. upside-down W-shape
C. spiral
D. upside-down U-shapes
E. W on its side
F. upside-down V-shapes
G. diamond inside a square

_____ 2.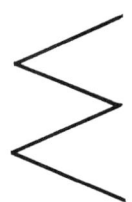

_____ 3.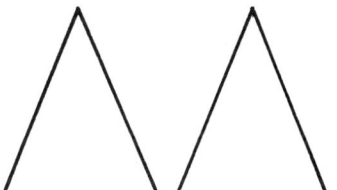

_____ 4.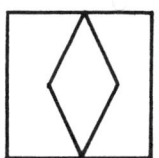

_____ 5.

LINES, SHAPES, AND DESIGNS

What's My Design?

Name _____

Look at the designs below. Use direction words and shape words to describe each of them. Write your descriptions in the blanks on the right. The first one is done for you.

1. 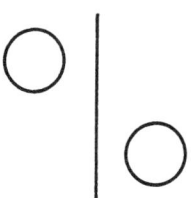   There is a circle at the top left side of a vertical straight line and another circle on the bottom right side.

2.    _____
   _____
   _____

3.    _____
   _____
   _____

4.    _____
   _____
   _____

5.    _____
   _____
   _____

LINES, SHAPES, AND DESIGNS

How About These Designs?

Name _____

Look at the designs below. Use direction words and shape words to describe each of them. Write your descriptions in the blanks on the right.

1. 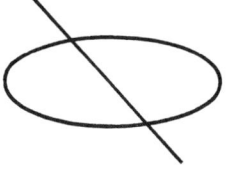   _____
   _____
   _____

2. 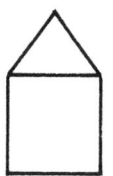   _____
   _____
   _____

3.    _____
   _____
   _____

4.    _____
   _____
   _____

5. 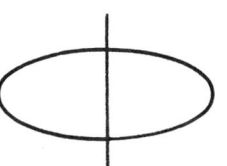   _____
   _____
   _____

Which Design Is It?

Name _____

Here are some fun designs to use in a barrier game.

1.  2.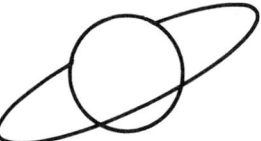

3.  4.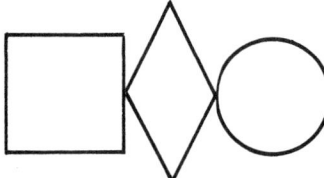

5.  6.

7. 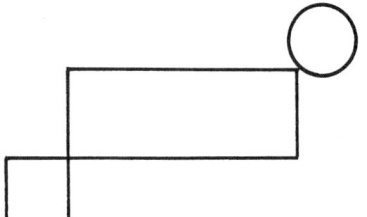 8.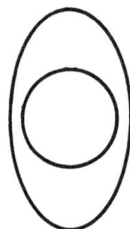

LINES, SHAPES, AND DESIGNS

Listen and Choose

Name _____

Here are some fun designs to use in a barrier game.

1.    2.

3.    4.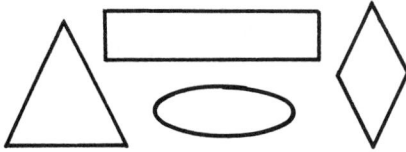

5.    6.

7.    8.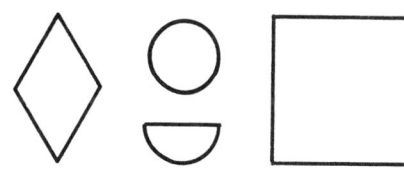

LINES, SHAPES, AND DESIGNS

Design Search

Name _____

Here are some fun designs to use in a barrier game.

1.

2.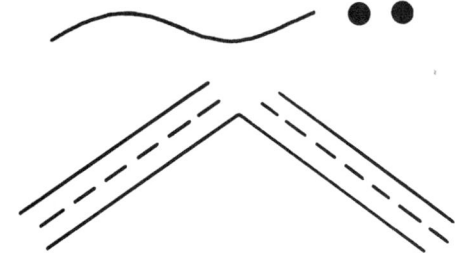

3.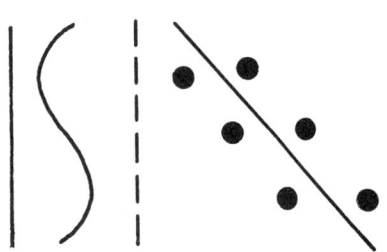

4.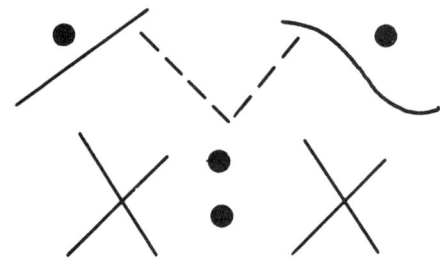

5.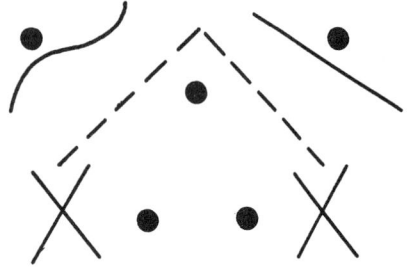

6.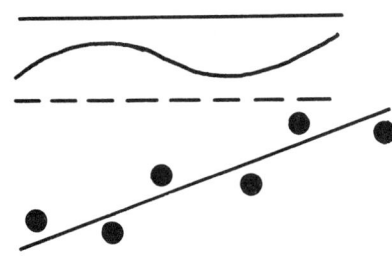

7.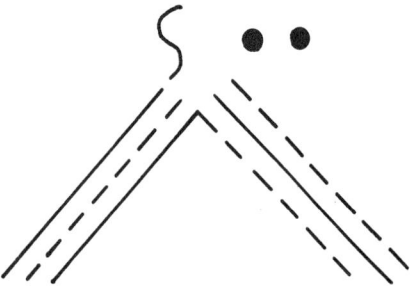

8.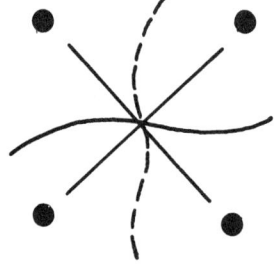

LINES, SHAPES, AND DESIGNS

Mazes, Maps, and Graphs

Throughout their school years, students are expected to follow directions. They are asked to put their names "on the top left side of the paper," to return completed assignments to "the third box from the bottom," and to learn how to draw and interpret graphs. As they get older, students must give directions to their homes, to rooms in their schools, and must master the geography of the Earth. Many language-impaired students have difficulty with these kinds of tasks, often giving directions by gesturing, pointing, and using phrases, such as "Go up there and then turn that way." These students have not mastered the technique of using landmarks to pinpoint locations, often have difficulty with left-right distinction, and rarely use directional terms appropriately.

Barrier activities using mazes and maps reinforce students' abilities to give and follow directions. Since there are several paths to reach the goal, the speaker must be specific and use landmarks to guide his listeners through the maze or map. If instructions are given and followed correctly, all students finish at the same location. Demonstrate how specific language makes the task easier for both speaker and listener. For example, rephrase a student's instruction of "go on up and turn that way" to "go straight up past three openings and turn right."

The graphs provide the students with additional practice using directional terminology. Since graphs are difficult for many students, the instructor may need to teach how to use the coordinates on a graph. In this series of exercises, if instructions are given and followed appropriately, all students finish with the same shaded pattern.

Instructions

Choose one of the mazes, maps, or graphs on pages 34 through 44. Place a barrier between the students. Give each student a copy of the activity sheet. When using graphs, the speaker has the finished picture and the listeners have copies of the blank graph, page 44. Specific instructions for each worksheet are found on pages 31 through 32.

Step 1: Play the speaker's role. Once the students are successful following directions, proceed to Step 2.

Step 2: Designate one of the students as the speaker and have him direct the others along the correct path.

Step 3: Once the students are successful switching speaker/listener roles with graphs, have them create their own designs to describe to the others.

Whenever students are speakers, transcribe the sequence of their directions. Use these transcriptions to compare the completed figures for accuracy. Discuss the reasons for any differences.

Consider substituting the terms *north, south, east,* and *west* for *up, down, left,* and *right* for students with a history of difficulty with *left* and *right*. Whenever appropriate, let the students use Direction Reminder A (page 14), Direction Reminder B (page 15), or Direction Reminder C (page 33), as a guide to the correct terms to use.

Follow the Dots, page 34

Place a star at the dot where the speaker will begin. The speaker instructs the others to move a certain distance and direction (e.g., "two dots north" or "four dots up").

Variation: Give a completed figure to the students. Have them work together to figure out what directions need to be given to draw that figure.

Which Number Is It?, page 35

The speaker secretly chooses a number as his destination. Then, he instructs the others along the path he takes. He may pass through other numbers, but he may not cross any thick, black lines.

Which Picture Is It?, page 36

The speaker secretly chooses a picture as his destination. Then, he instructs the others along the path he takes. He may pass through other pictures, but he may not cross any black lines.

Listen and Do, page 37

Have the students cut the map apart on the dotted lines. The speaker rearranges his pieces to form a new map and directs the others to put their pieces together in the same way.

Which Way?, page 38

The speaker explains the path the car would take to a chosen landmark, choosing alternate routes in case of roadblocks (e.g., the bridge is out or the train blocks the road).

A Drive in the Country, page 39

The speaker explains his route from one place to another.

All Graphs, pages 40 through 44

The speaker uses the graph coordinates to tell the others how to duplicate a message or figure (e.g., "shade in 7G to 7K") on a blank graph.

Core Vocabulary

bottom	opening
corner	over
destination	past
dot	path
dotted	right
down	shade
east	south
figure	southeast
go	southwest
graph	space
landmark	straight
left	thick
map	top
maze	turn
middle	under
north	up
northeast	west
northwest	

Direction Reminder C

Name _____

Use this sheet to help you remember the compass directions.

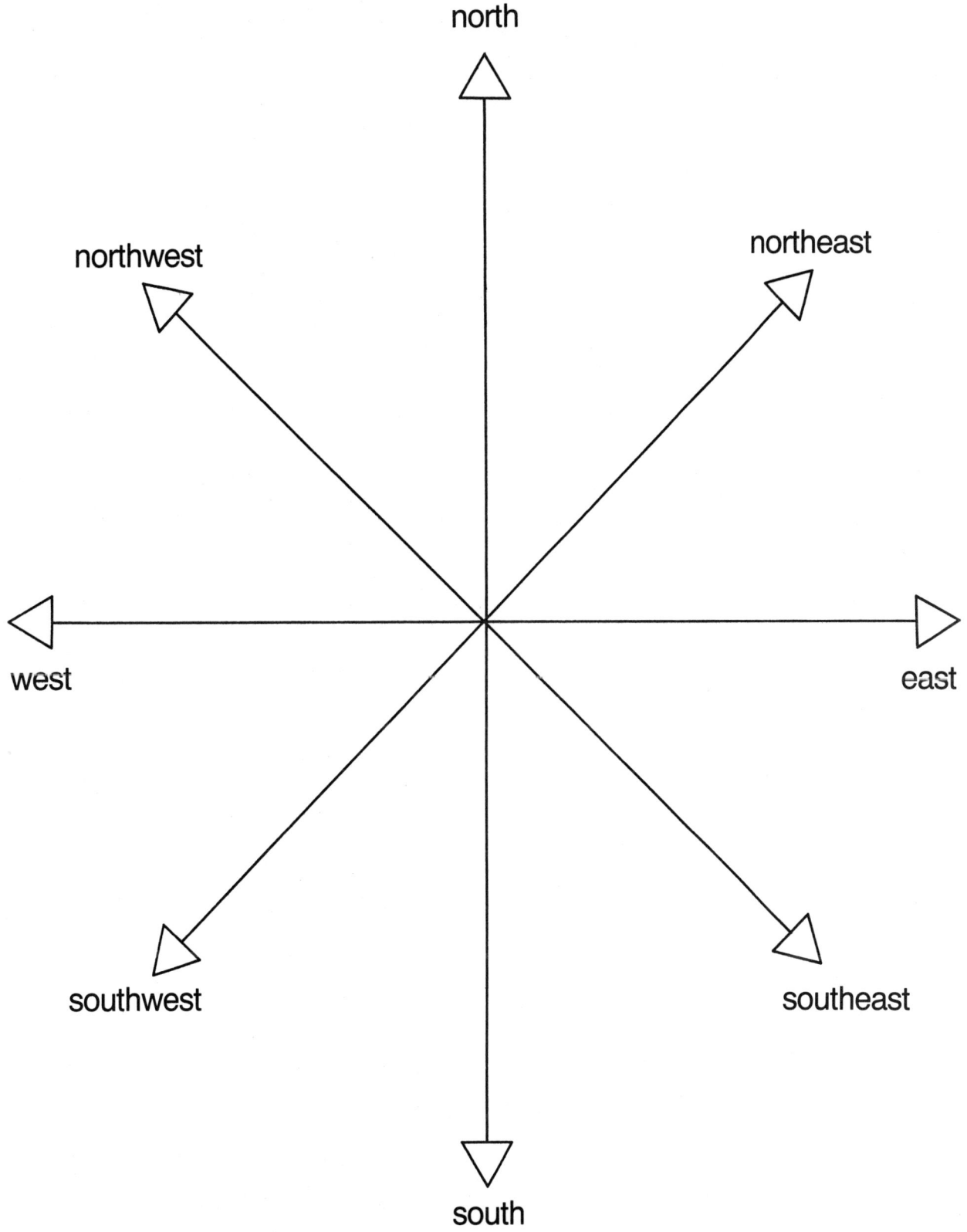

Follow the Dots

Name _____

Here is a page full of dots to follow for fun as you listen or describe.

Which Number Is It?

Name _____

Find your way through this maze as you listen or describe.

MAZES, MAPS, AND GRAPHS

Which Picture Is It?

Name _____

Find the right picture as you listen or describe.

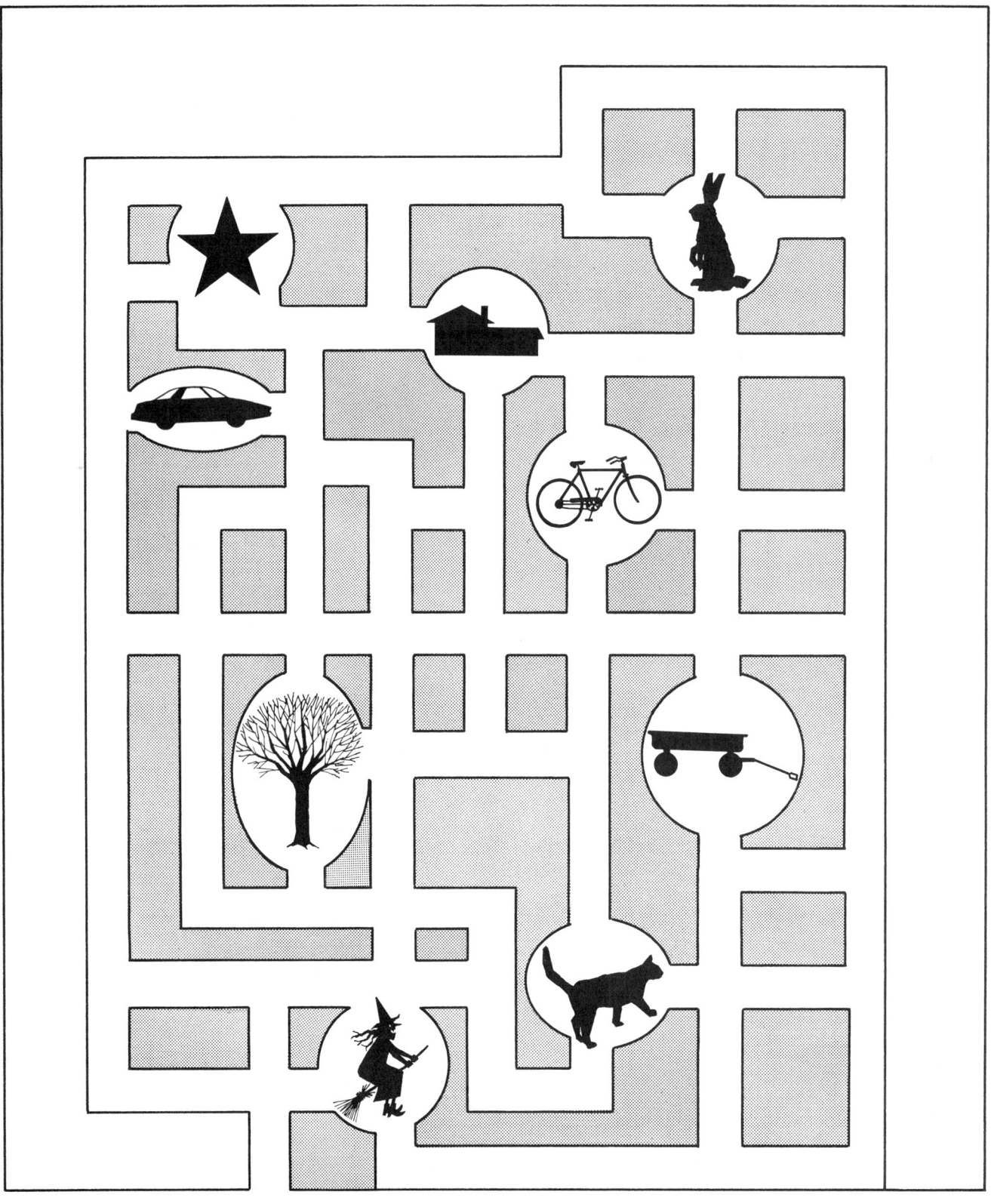

Start

MAZES, MAPS, AND GRAPHS · 36 · Copyright © 1987 LinguiSystems, Inc.

Listen and Do

Name _____

Here is a puzzle to cut apart and put back together as you listen or describe.

MAZES, MAPS, AND GRAPHS

Copyright © 1987 LinguiSystems, Inc.

Which Way? Name _____

Here is a city map to use for fun as you listen or describe.

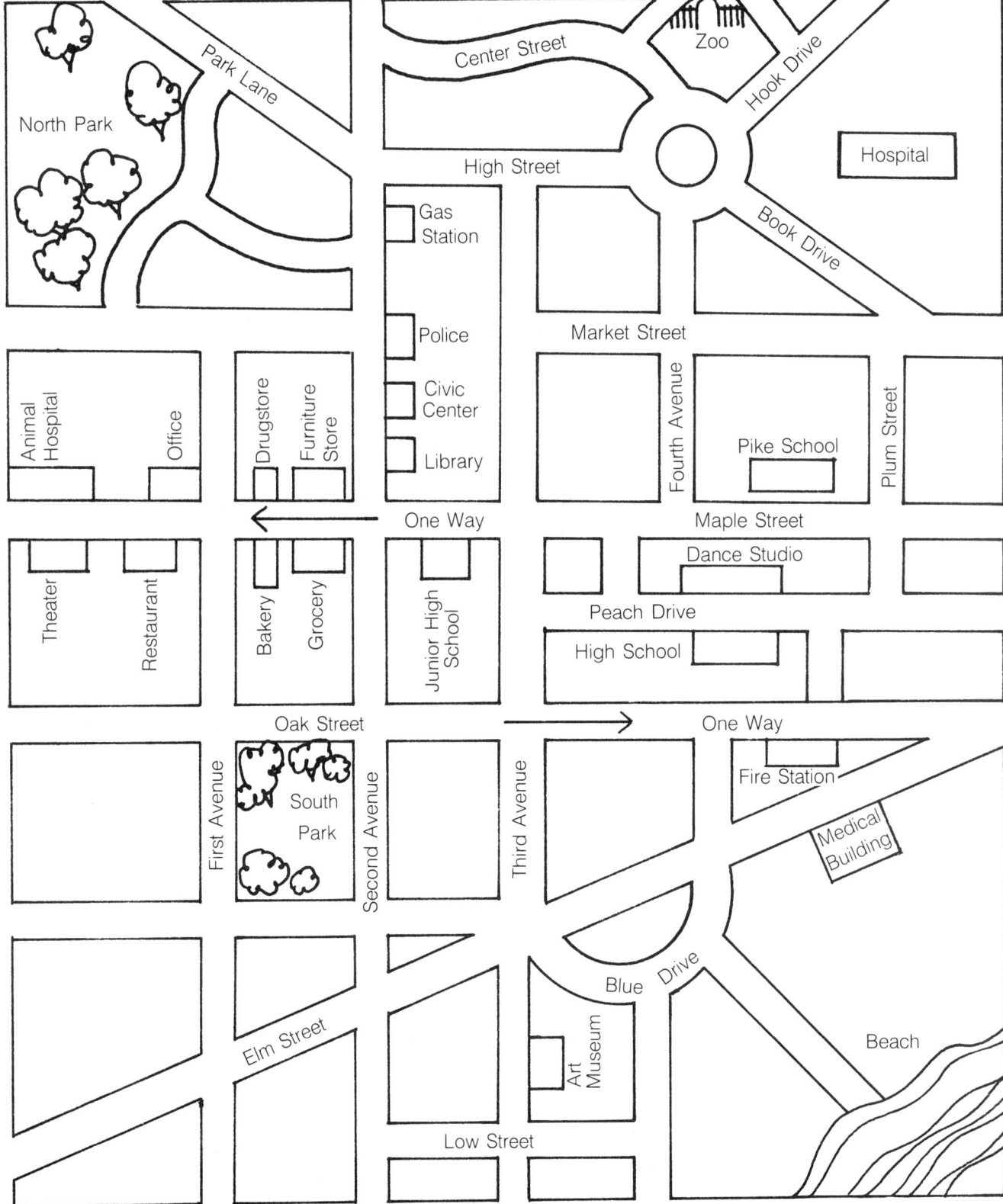

MAZES, MAPS, AND GRAPHS

A Drive in the Country

Name _____

Here is a country map to use for fun as you listen or describe.

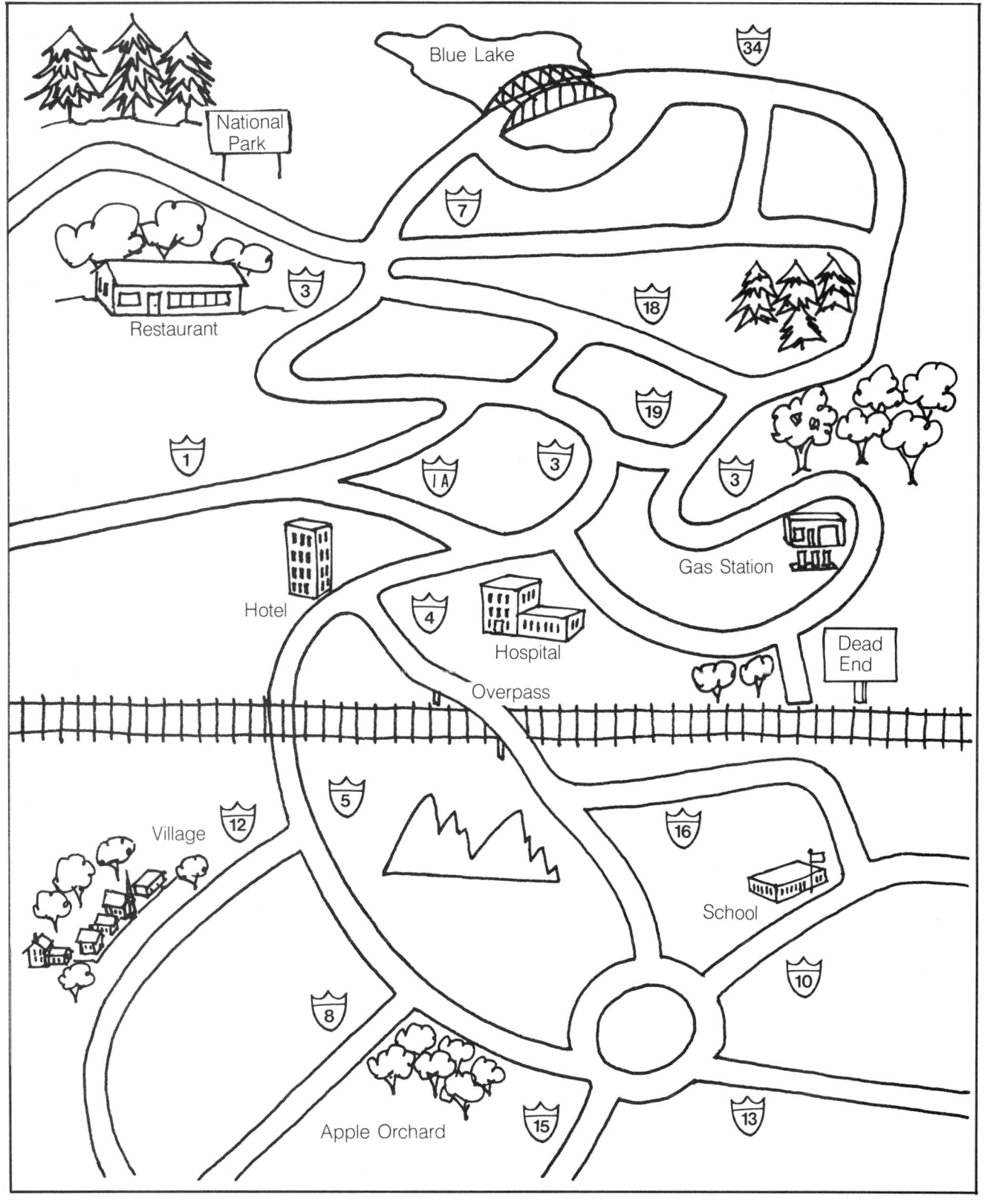

Give the Message

Name _____

Use this graph to practice giving directions.

What Will You Say?

Name _____

Use this graph to practice giving directions.

Rockets Away!

Name _____

Use this graph to practice giving directions.

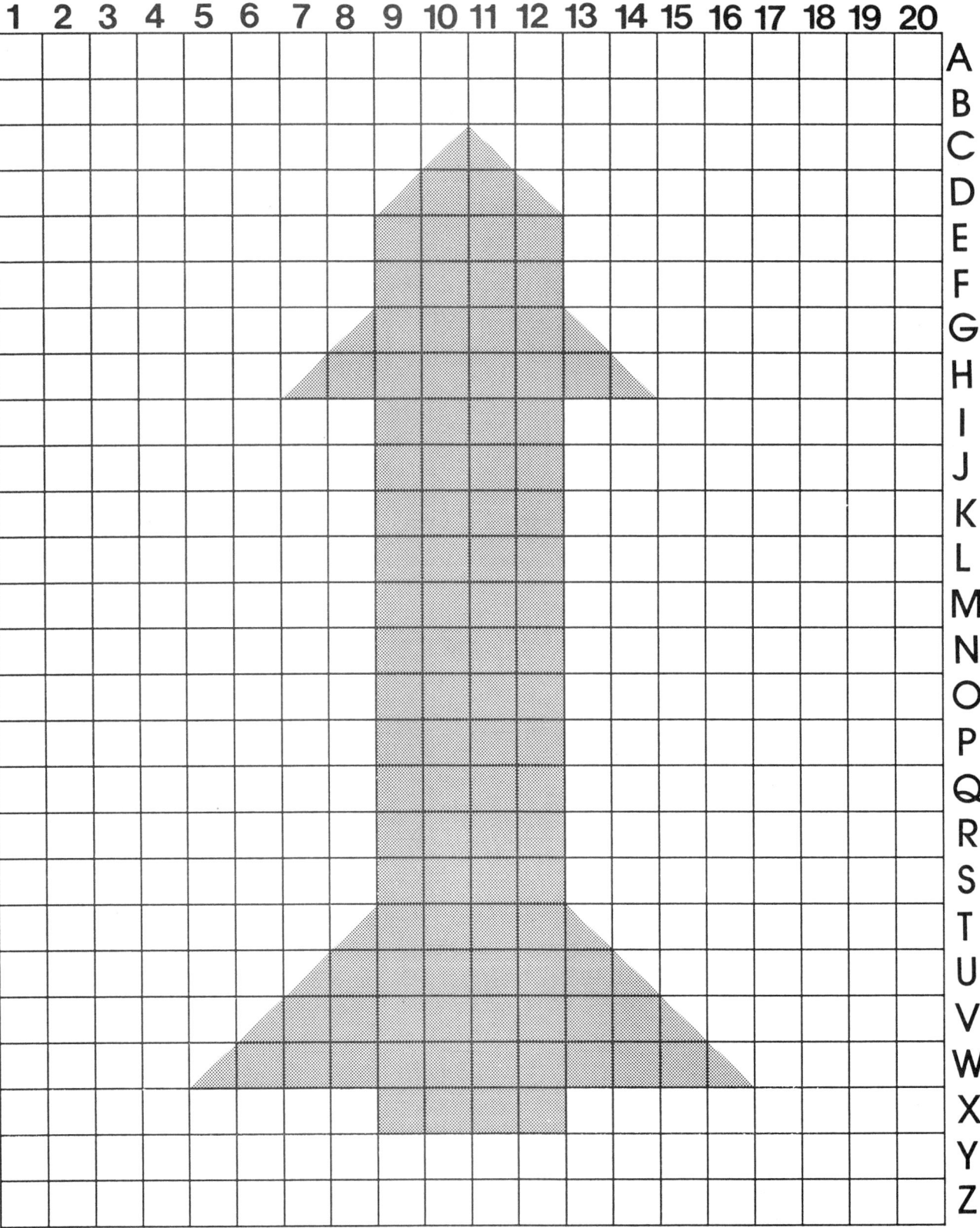

MAZES, MAPS, AND GRAPHS

Copyright © 1987 LinguiSystems, Inc.

Home Sweet Home

Name _____

Use this graph to practice giving directions.

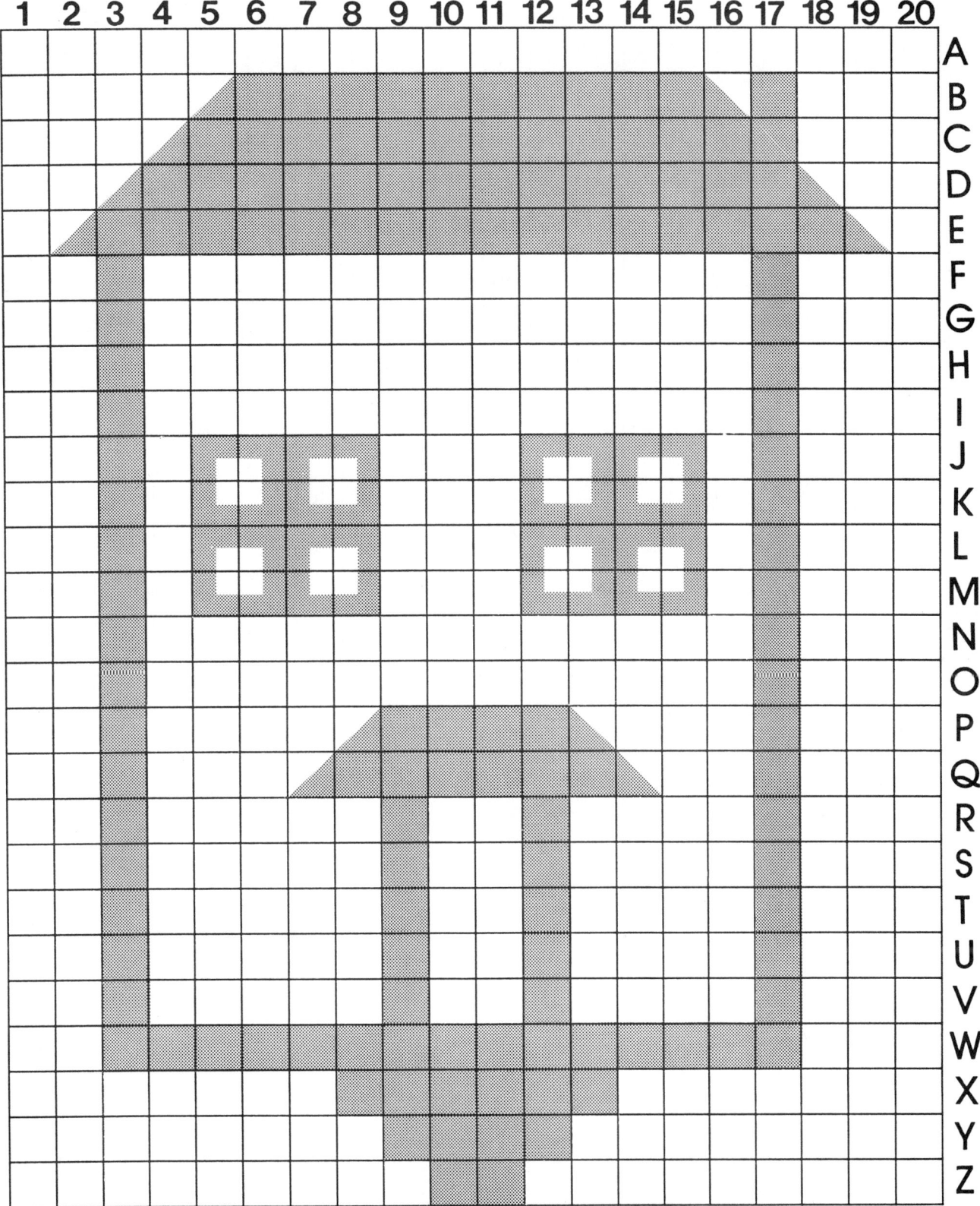

MAZES, MAPS, AND GRAPHS 43 Copyright © 1987 LinguiSystems, Inc.

Make Your Own Graph Picture!

Name _____

Use this graph as you listen or describe.

Cut and Place

The activities in this unit reinforce the shape and directional concepts taught in the worksheet units of *Lines, Shapes, and Designs* and *Mazes, Maps, and Graphs*. These activities also add variety and interest to the barrier tasks.

For some students, manipulating shapes to achieve the desired picture is easier than drawing the design from verbal instructions alone. These students may learn more quickly with the hands-on approach of these activities.

The language skills necessary to succeed in these barrier tasks are similar to those required in art projects and classroom listening activities. Listening as well as language skills should improve with mastery of these activities.

Instructions

Choose one of the Cut and Place activity sheets on pages 46 through 51. Place a barrier between the students. Have each student cut out the associated shapes.

Step 1: Using the completed picture, describe the placement of the shapes so the students can duplicate it.

Step 2: Have the students take turns playing the speaker.

Core Vocabulary

above	rectangle
beside	shape
bottom	small
circle	square
diamond	top
large	triangle
over	under

Which Shapes Go Where?   Name _____

Explain how to place these shapes to make a sailboat.

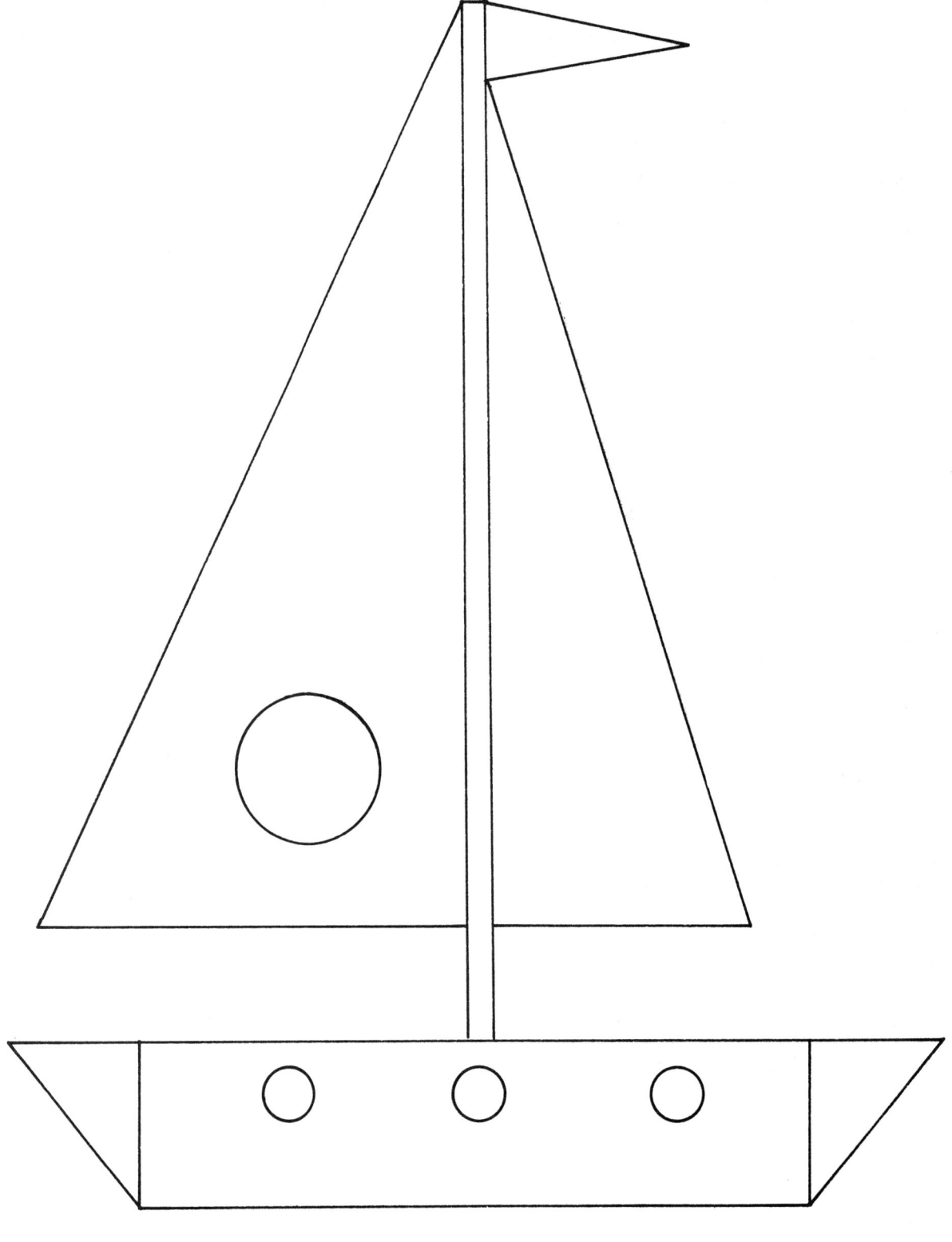

CUT AND PLACE

Which Shapes Go Where?, continued   Name _____

Cut these shapes apart. Then, listen carefully to the speaker. Follow the speaker's directions to put these shapes together.

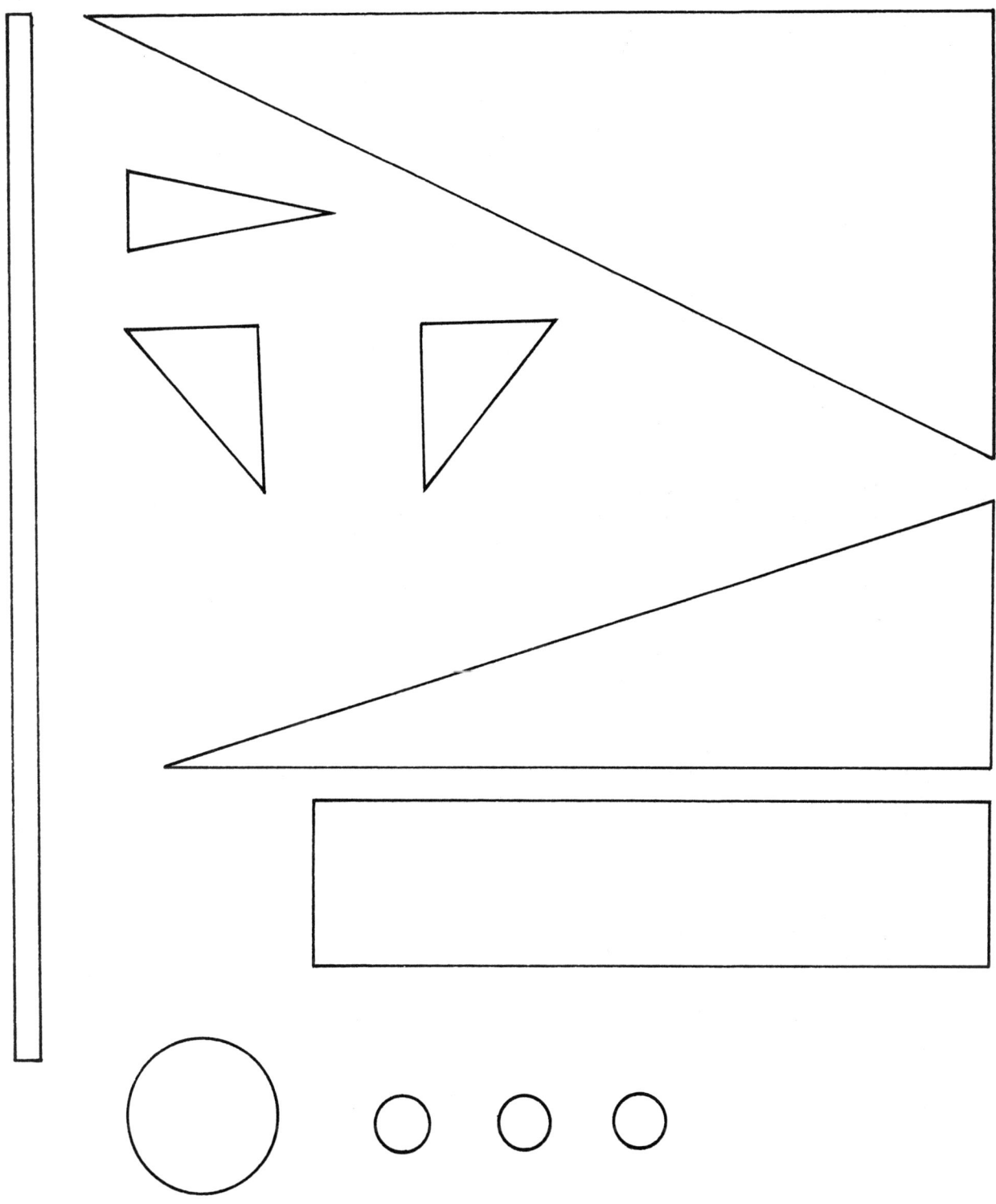

CUT AND PLACE   47   Copyright © 1987 LinguiSystems, Inc.

Shape Sort

Name _____

Explain how to place these shapes to make a race car.

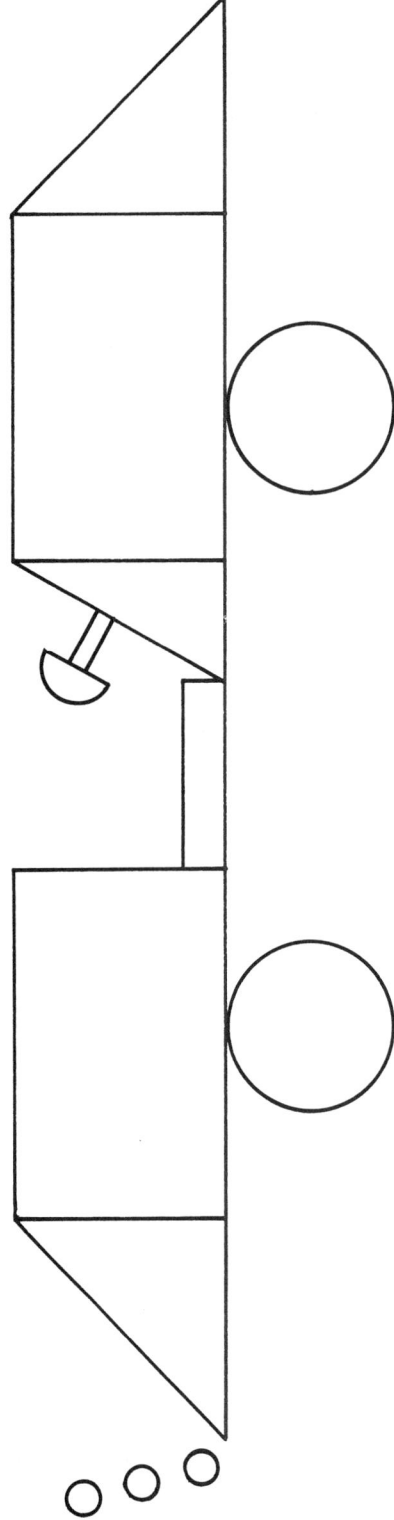

CUT AND PLACE — 48 — Copyright © 1987 LinguiSystems, Inc.

Shape Sort, continued   Name _____

Cut these shapes apart. Then, listen carefully to the speaker. Follow the speaker's directions to put these shapes together.

CUT AND PLACE   49   Copyright © 1987 LinguiSystems, Inc.

Listen and Place

Name _____

Explain how to place these shapes to make a church.

CUT AND PLACE

Listen and Place, continued   Name _____

Cut these shapes apart. Then, listen carefully to the speaker. Follow the directions to put these shapes together.

CUT AND PLACE   51   Copyright © 1987 LinguiSystems, Inc.

Scene Descriptions

The activities in this unit provide the student with strategies for organizing information to describe a scene. Following the presented sequence of worksheets, the student learns to begin by naming the topic (e.g., *a farm, a birthday party, a playground,* etc.), and then to use directional terms (e.g., *left, right, middle,* etc.) to locate the details of the scene. Since this strategy of going from general to specific information is widespread in school learning, mastery of this skill can improve academic performance as well as general communication skills.

Instructions

Proceed through the worksheets of this unit in order. Hand out the first worksheet. Read, or have the student read, the instructions on each worksheet and fill out the worksheet accordingly. Each of these worksheets can be done as an oral or a written task.

Provide guidance whenever necessary to help the student proceed from general to specific information and to choose the correct terms to locate the details of each scene.

Core Vocabulary

All Scenes, pages 55 through 64

above	inside
background	left
beside	middle
between	on
in	right
in front of	

Fill It Up, page 55

car	pump
door	service bay
gas station	window

Tell Me About It, page 56

barn	pig
chicken	pond
duck	road
farm	silo

Tell Me More, page 57

circus	lion
clown	tent
elephant	

What's the Scene?, page 58

hopscotch	slide
playground	swing
sandbox	

Finish Up!, page 59

bathroom	sink
mirror	toilet
rug	toilet paper
shower	tub

Where Is It?, page 60

bird	
cage	pet store
cat	snake
mice	tree

What Do You See?, page 61

bedroom	table
far	twin bed
lamp	wall

What's Happening?, page 62

banner	children
birthday	party
cake	presents
chairs	

Tell Me All About It!, page 63

cage
monkey
popcorn

tiger
zoo

Fill Me In!, page 64

hill
lake

picnic table
sailboat

Fill It Up

Name _____

Describe the picture below. Choose words from the box to fill in the blanks.

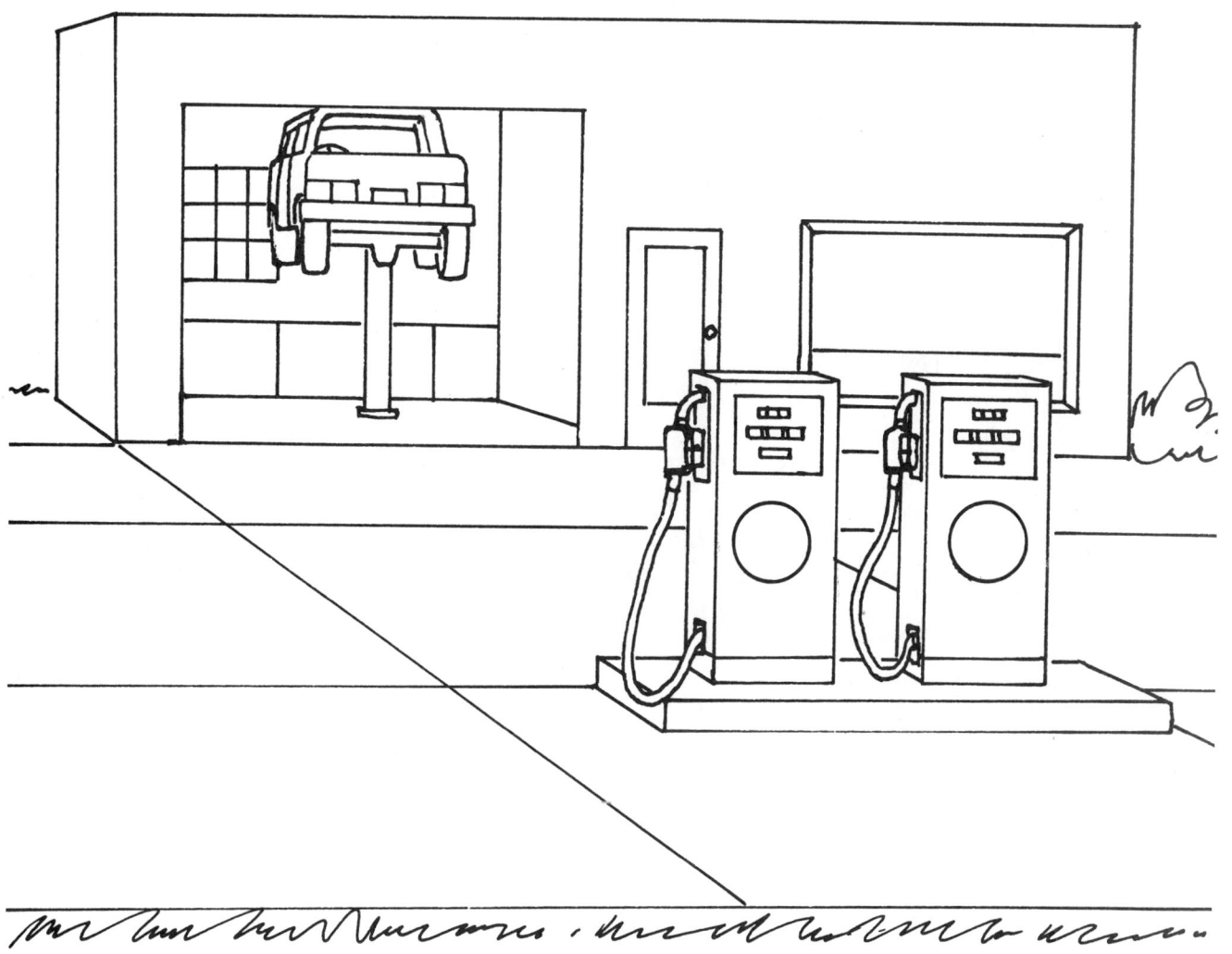

| left | front | inside | right |

This is a gas station. Two pumps are in _____ of the window on the _____ side. A service bay is on the _____ side. There is a car _____ the service bay.

SCENE DESCRIPTIONS

Tell Me About It

Name _____

Describe the picture below. Choose words from the box to fill in the blanks.

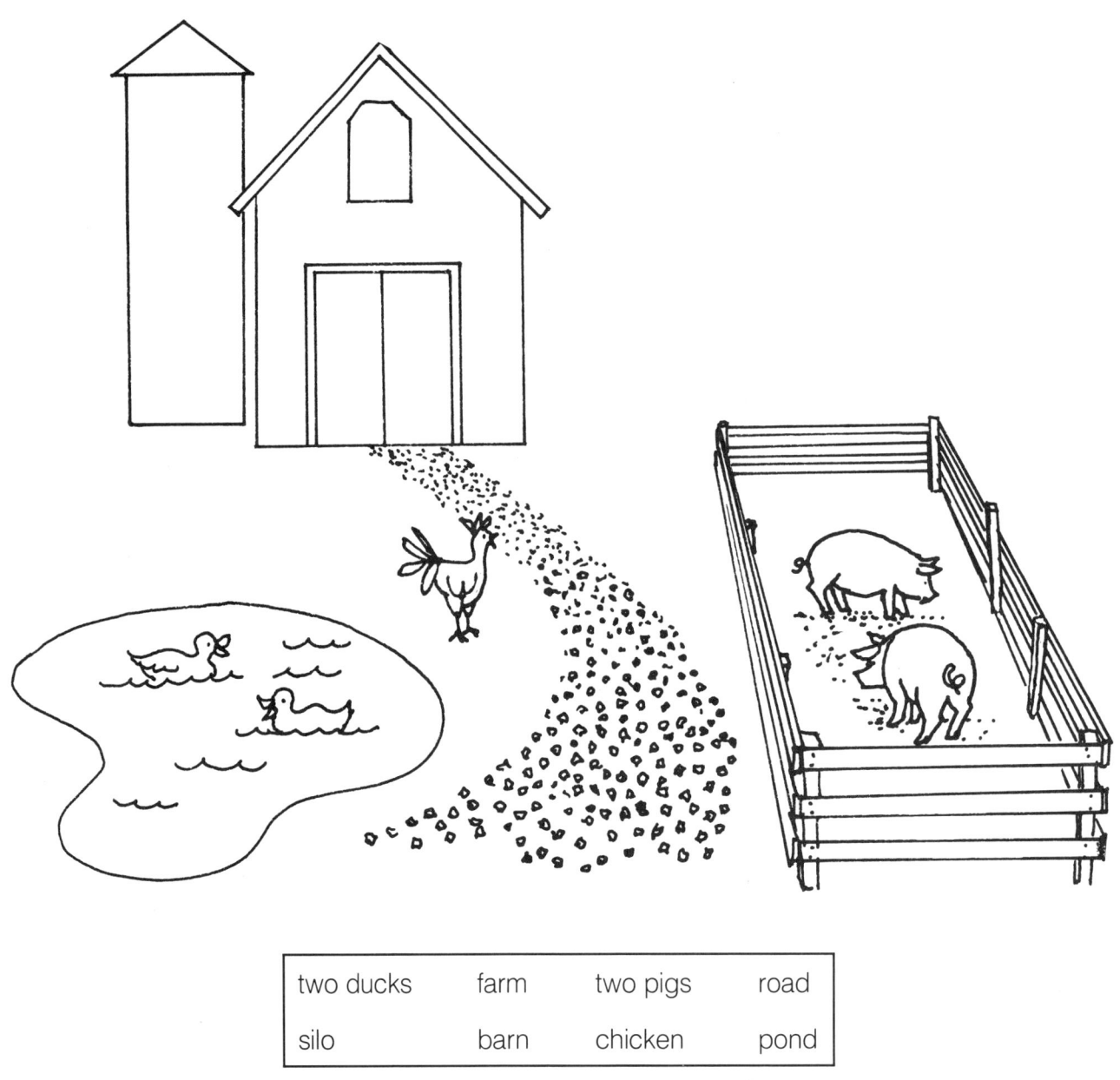

two ducks	farm	two pigs	road
silo	barn	chicken	pond

This is a picture of a _____. A _____ and a

_____ are in the background. _____ are on the right

side. _____ are on the left side. In front of the barn is a

_____ with a _____ beside it.

SCENE DESCRIPTIONS

Tell Me More

Name _____

Describe the picture below. Choose words from the box to fill in the blanks. Some words may be used twice.

| between | right | front | clown |
| circus | left | elephant | lion |

This is a _____. A _____ is on the _____ side. On the _____ side is a big _____. It is in _____ of the tent. A funny _____ is _____ the _____ and the elephant.

SCENE DESCRIPTIONS

What's the Scene?

Name _____

Describe the picture below.   Fill in the blanks with the missing words.

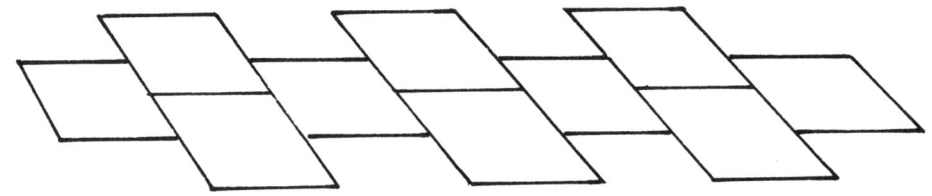

This is a _____.   There are _____ on the left side.

There is a _____ on the right side.   There is a _____ in

the middle.   The _____ is in the front.

SCENE DESCRIPTIONS

Finish Up!   Name _____

Describe the picture below. Fill in the blanks with the missing words.

This is a _____ . A sink is on the _____ side. It has a

mirror _____ it. A bathtub and a shower are on the

_____ . The toilet is _____ . A rug is

_____ .

SCENE DESCRIPTIONS

Where Is It?

Name _____

Describe the picture below. Fill in the blanks with the missing words.

This is a _____ . The _____ is wrapped around the tree on the left. The _____ is on the right. The _____ are in a cage on _____ of the _____ . The _____ is in a cage above the _____ .

SCENE DESCRIPTIONS   60   Copyright © 1987 LinguiSystems, Inc.

What Do You See?

Name _____

Describe this picture. First, tell what it is about. Then, tell more about the picture. Use words like *left, right, top,* and *side.*

_____
_____
_____
_____
_____

SCENE DESCRIPTIONS

Copyright © 1987 LinguiSystems, Inc.

What's Happening? Name _____

Describe this picture. First, tell what it is about. Then, tell how many children there are and tell where things are in the picture.

_____
_____
_____
_____
_____

SCENE DESCRIPTIONS

Tell Me All About It!   Name _____

Describe this picture. Tell the most important things and where they are.

_____
_____
_____
_____
_____

Fill Me In!

Name _____

Describe this picture.

_____
_____
_____
_____
_____

SCENE DESCRIPTIONS 64 Copyright © 1987 LinguiSystems, Inc.

Comparing through Similes

The objective of this unit is to teach students how to use their knowledge of common shapes and objects to help them communicate more effectively. Many language-impaired students overuse non-descriptive words such as *thing* and *stuff* because they do not know how to describe an object. Teaching these students to use similes to compare one thing to another encourages them to use fewer "empty" words.

These activities progress in difficulty by decreasing the amount of information provided to students. The initial activity requires students to match the shape or line with the appropriate description. Subsequent activities combine the shapes and lines to form familiar objects and the students learn to recognize the shapes of the individual parts. For example, they learn to see that the bird's beak is a triangle and the clown's mouth is a heart. As the activities progress, the students are required to use their imagination more, searching for a mental picture of a familiar object which looks like the part described. For example, students could describe a poodle's body as popcorn, a cotton ball, or a cloud. Successful completion of these activities results in less use of gestures and more specific use of descriptive language.

Instructions

Proceed through the worksheets of this unit in order. Hand out the first worksheet. Read, or have the student read, the instructions on each worksheet and fill out the worksheet accordingly. Each of these worksheets can be done as an oral or a written task.

Ideally, these excercises are remediation activities to be used as teaching rather than testing tasks. The objective is not to see which student gets the most "right" answers but rather, how much accurate descriptive language the students can generate. Encourage the students to brainstorm and to discuss reasons for the effectiveness or ineffectiveness of particular responses.

Core Vocabulary

acorn	lips
beak	mouth
bell-shaped	mushroom
body	nose
bowling pin	oval
button	pear
candy cane	popcorn
circle	rectangle
cloud	S-curve
cracker	shoe
crossed	spring
curls	square
doughnut	star
ear	stop sign
egg	stripes
eye	three
feet	triangle
fin	U-shaped
hair	wavy
half circle	wing
hamburger	wire
heart	zigzag
innertube	

What Does It Look Like?

Name _____

Look at the pictures below. Then, read the descriptions on the right. Match each picture to its description by writing letters in the blanks beside the pictures. Some pictures may have more than one correct description.

_____ 1.

It looks like _____ .

    A. an egg
    B. the bottom of a shoe
    C. a doughnut
    D. an innertube
_____ 2.
    E. a hamburger
    F. lips
    G. a pear
    H. a wire
    I. a curl
_____ 3.
    J. a spring

_____ 4.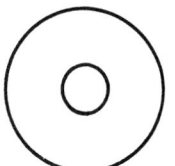

_____ 5.

COMPARING THROUGH SIMILES

What Could It Be?

Name _____

Look at the pictures below. Then, read the descriptions on the right. Match each picture to its description by writing letters in the blanks beside the pictures. Some pictures may have more than one correct description.

_____ 1.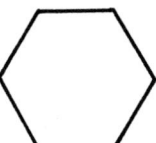

It looks like _____ .

    A. a candy cane

    B. a cloud

    C. popcorn

    D. a bowling pin

_____ 2.

    E. a stop sign

    F. a bell

    G. an acorn

    H. cotton candy

    I. a hat

_____ 3.

    J. a chicken leg

_____ 4.

_____ 5.

COMPARING THROUGH SIMILES

What Shape Is It?

Name _____

Can you find the different shapes in these pictures? Tell how each picture looks by filling in each blank with the correct shape.

1.

    The body is like _____.
    The eyes are like _____.
    The mouth is like _____.
    The fins are like _____.

2.

    The ears are like _____.
    The eyes are like _____.
    The mouth is like _____.
    The nose is like _____.
    The hair is like _____.

3.

    The eye is like _____.
    The beak is like _____.
    The wing is like _____.
    The feet are like _____.

COMPARING THROUGH SIMILES   Copyright © 1987 LinguiSystems, Inc.

More Shapes!

Name _____

Can you find the different shapes in these pictures? Tell how each picture looks by describing the shapes you see.

1.

   The nose is like _____.

   The hair is like _____.

   The body is like _____.

   The feet are like _____.

   The tail is like _____.

   The eyes are like _____.

2.

   _____
   _____
   _____
   _____

3.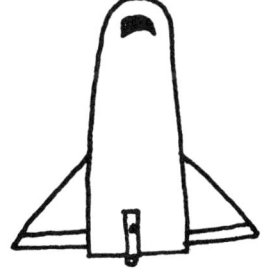

   _____
   _____
   _____
   _____

Even More Shapes!

Name _____

Can you find the different shapes in these pictures? Tell how each picture looks by describing the shapes you see.

1.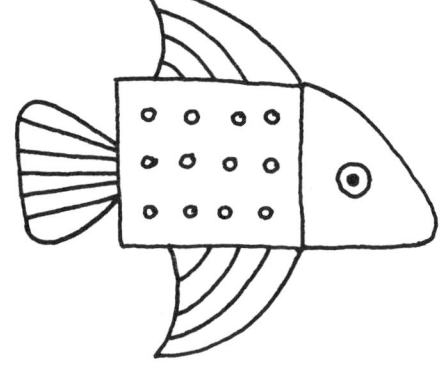

   _____
   _____
   _____
   _____

2.

   _____
   _____
   _____
   _____

3.

   _____
   _____
   _____
   _____

COMPARING THROUGH SIMILES

Picture These!

Name _____

Make each of these designs into a picture of something. Tell how you did it.

Example: An  could be an  or a

                        oval   eyeball   flying saucer

COMPARING THROUGH SIMILES

Focusing on Important Features

This unit not only teaches students to use descriptive language, but to use it in a specific manner by focusing on the most important details. Students learn to recognize the most important characteristics of objects and to disregard minor details which often lead to confusion or misinterpretation in the communication process. For example, when younger students begin playing guessing games and are asked to describe a picture or an object, they often state color or size as the first clue, whether or not color or size is significant. As students mature in cognitive and language skills, they learn to discriminate between significant and insignificant characteristics. For example, when describing *scissors,* a student who has learned to be specific in his use of language begins with "It's something that cuts" instead of "It's silver."

Language-impaired students are often slow in learning this discrimination process. They continue to focus on the most concrete, visible characteristics (e.g., color and size) rather than the most significant features. During conversations, they frequently fail to make their pronoun referents clear. They may also give redundant or insufficient information, are likely to change topics without warning, and in general, leave the listener confused. The listener must then ask questions for clarification. With some students, even questioning does not result in a clear communication.

The activities in this unit progress in difficulty by decreasing the support provided for students. Certain activities demonstrate that even though some information is true, it may not be important to the communication. For example, a wagon may be red, but color does not contribute to the essence of a wagon. On the other hand, color is significant when describing a banana.

Instructions

Proceed through the worksheets of this unit in order. Hand out the first worksheet. Read, or have the student read, the instructions on each worksheet and fill out the worksheet accordingly. Each of these worksheets can be done as an oral or a written task.

Core Vocabulary

What's Important?, page 75

arm	lamp
bicycle	leg
button	man
chair	mustache
dial	phone
ear	shade
elephant	trunk
eyes	wheel

What's Missing?, page 76

book	portable
channel selector	print
console	rose
fish	shark
flower	shoe
laces	sole
loafer	tail fin
petal	television
picture	tulip

Necessary Details, page 77

animal	lead
babies	listening
beak	motor
big	pencil
bird	point
blue	ride
break	shape
car	talking
color	telephone
communication	vehicle
dial tone	wing
fast	wires
feathers	words
fender	write

What Makes It?, page 78

appliance	mix
blender	nail
book	noisy
chair	page
communication	picture
cushions	pounding
electrical	printed
food	rock
furniture	sit
hammer	size
handle	soft
hard	store
kitchen	tall
leg	tool

Zero In, page 79

apple	red
bus	seed
eggbeater	table
fruit	television
green	tree
grow	yellow

Fill It In, page 80

bicycle	knife
communication	lamp
computer	screen
electrical	tiger
keyboard	

Can You Define It?, page 81

(See **Zero In**, page 79)

More Definitions, page 82

(See **Fill It In**, page 80)

What's Important?

Name _____

Look at the three pictures in each row. Circle the picture which is missing something important.

Example:

1.

2.

3.

4.

5.

What's Missing?

Name _____

Look at the three pictures in each row. Circle the picture which is missing something important.

Example:

1.

2.

3.

4.

5.

FOCUSING ON IMPORTANT FEATURES

Necessary Details

Name _____

Look at each picture on the left. Then, circle the most important features about the picture.

1.  A bird _____ .

   a. is blue   d. is an animal
   b. has wings   e. has feathers
   c. has babies   f. has a beak

2. 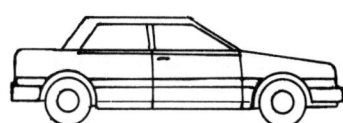 A car _____ .

   a. has fenders   d. is any color
   b. is big and fast e. is for riding in
   c. is a vehicle   f. has a motor

3. 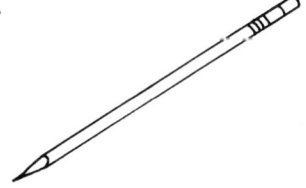 A pencil _____ .

   a. is yellow   d. has words on it
   b. has a point   e. has lead
   c. is used to write with f. can break

4.  A telephone _____ .

   a. can be any color   d. is for communication
   b. has wires   e. can be any shape
   c. is for talking and listening   f. has a dial tone

FOCUSING ON IMPORTANT FEATURES   Copyright © 1987 LinguiSystems, Inc.

What Makes It?   Name _____

Look at each picture on the left. Then, circle the most important features about the picture.

1. 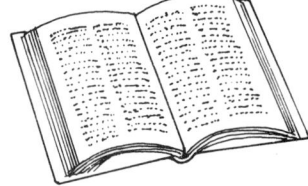   A book _____ .

    a. has pages   d. is printed

    b. has pictures   e. is for communication

    c. can be any size   f. can be hard or soft

2.    A hammer _____ .

    a. is a tool   d. is found in stores

    b. is used with nails   e. has a handle

    c. is for pounding   f. can be any size

3. 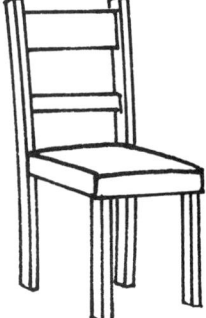   A chair _____ .

    a. can rock   d. is a piece of furniture

    b. has legs   e. is used for sitting

    c. can be soft or hard   f. can have cushions

4.    A blender _____ .

    a. is tall   d. mixes food

    b. is an appliance   e. is electrical

    c. is noisy   f. is used in the kitchen

FOCUSING ON IMPORTANT FEATURES

Zero In

Name _____

Look at each picture on the left. Then, write the most important features beside it. Fill in as many blanks as you can. The first one is done for you.

1.
   a. An apple is a fruit.
   b. It has seeds.
   c. It can be green, yellow, or red.
   d. An apple grows on trees.

2.
   a. _____
   b. _____
   c. _____
   d. _____

3.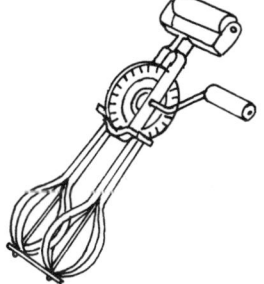
   a. _____
   b. _____
   c. _____
   d. _____

4.
   a. _____
   b. _____
   c. _____
   d. _____

5.
   a. _____
   b. _____
   c. _____
   d. _____

FOCUSING ON IMPORTANT FEATURES

Fill It In

Name _____

Look at each picture on the left. Then, write the most important features beside it. Fill in as many blanks as you can. The first one is done for you.

1.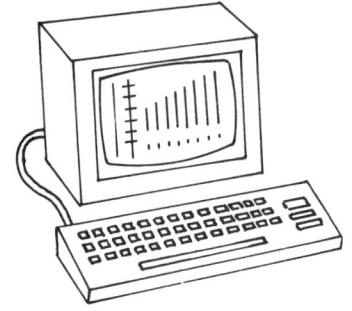
   a. A computer is for communication.
   b. It has a keyboard.
   c. It has a screen.
   d. A computer is electrical.

2.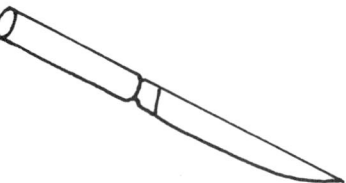
   a. _____
   b. _____
   c. _____
   d. _____

3.
   a. _____
   b. _____
   c. _____
   d. _____

4.
   a. _____
   b. _____
   c. _____
   d. _____

5.
   a. _____
   b. _____
   c. _____
   d. _____

Can You Define It?

Name _____

Using your answers for Zero In, page 79, write a definition for each of the words below. The first one is done for you.

1. apple
   a. _An apple is a fruit._
   b. _It has seeds._
   c. _It can be green, yellow, or red._
   d. _An apple grows on trees._

   An apple is a fruit that grows on trees. It can be green, yellow, or red and has seeds.

2. A television _____

3. An eggbeater _____

4. A bus _____

5. A table _____

FOCUSING ON IMPORTANT FEATURES

More Definitions

Name _____

Using your answers for Fill It In, page 80, write a definition for each of the words below. The first one is done for you.

1. computer
   a. A computer is for communication.
   b. It has a keyboard.
   c. It has a screen.
   d. A computer is electrical.

   A computer is used for communication. It runs on electricity and has a keyboard and a screen.

2. A knife _____

3. A tiger _____

4. A bicycle _____

5. A lamp _____

Picture Pair Discrimination

Select picture pairs from the list below to help students focus on the discriminating features between similar items. Present pairs of pictures, pages 85 through 88, which are similar except for one or two attributes. Have the students describe one of the pictures using as few clues as possible.

Picture Pairs		Some Discriminating Features
cherry	apple	A cherry is little. An apple is big.
scissors	tongs	Scissors cut. Tongs pick up things.
rake	hoe	A rake is used to gather up leaves in piles. A hoe is used to dig up weeds.
bicycle	tricycle	A bicycle has two wheels. A tricycle has three wheels.
mug	glass	A mug has a handle. A glass does not have a handle.
pitchfork	dinner fork	A dinner fork is for eating. A pitchfork is for picking up and tossing hay.
firefighter	police officer	A firefighter puts out fires. A police officer enforces the law.
swing	seesaw	A swing moves back and forth. A seesaw goes up and down.
helicopter	plane	A helicopter has a propeller on top. A plane has its propeller in front.
waterfall	shower	A waterfall is made of natural waters. A shower comes out of man-made pipes.
pen	pencil	A pen writes with ink. A pencil writes with lead.
chair	couch	A chair is for one person. A couch is for more than one person.
hairbrush	toothbrush	A hairbrush is for hair. A toothbrush is for teeth.
house	barn	People live in a house. Animals live in a barn.
picnic basket	box	A picnic basket is for carrying a lunch. A box can carry many different things.
fairy	butterfly	A fairy is make-believe. A butterfly is real.
ghost	cloud	A ghost is not real. You can see a cloud.
mask	eyeglasses	A mask is a disguise worn over the face or eyes. Eyeglasses help us to see better.
shoe	slipper	Shoes are worn inside and outside of the house. Slippers are for inside.
button	doughnut	A button is a fastener for clothing. A doughnut is food.
paints	crayons	Paints are wet. Crayons are dry.

Picture Pair Discrimination, continued

Picture Pairs		Some Discriminating Features
air conditioner	fan	An air conditioner cools and blows air. A fan blows room air.
radio	television	We can listen to information on the radio. We can listen and watch television.
window	door	We look out a window. We walk through a door.
canoe	rowboat	You paddle a canoe. You row a rowboat.
compass	wall clock	A compass tells directions. A wall clock tells time.
movie projector	video camera	A movie projector shows movies on a screen. A video camera takes pictures to show on television.
escalator	stairs	An escalator moves. Stairs are stationary.
leopard	tiger	A leopard has spots. A tiger has stripes.
station wagon	car (sedan)	A station wagon has extra space in back. A car (sedan) has a trunk.
book	magazine	A book can have a hard cover. A magazine has a soft cover.
kangaroo	rabbit	A kangaroo is big. A rabbit is small.

What's Different?

Name _____

Use these picture pairs to talk about differences.

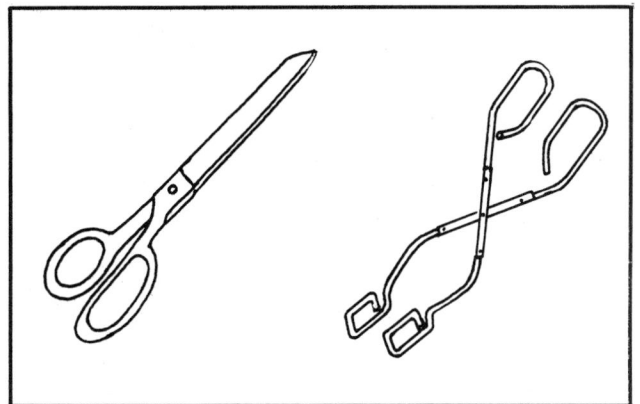
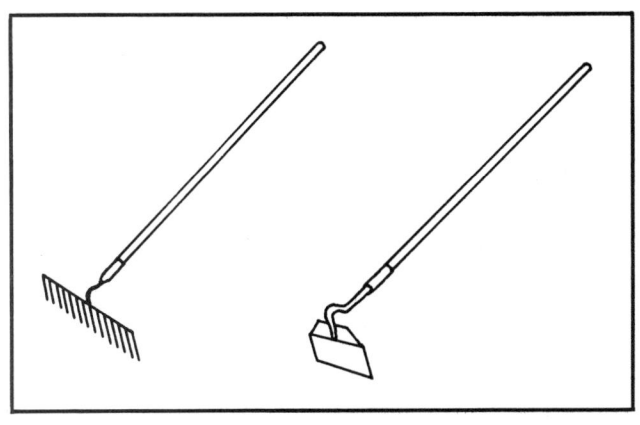

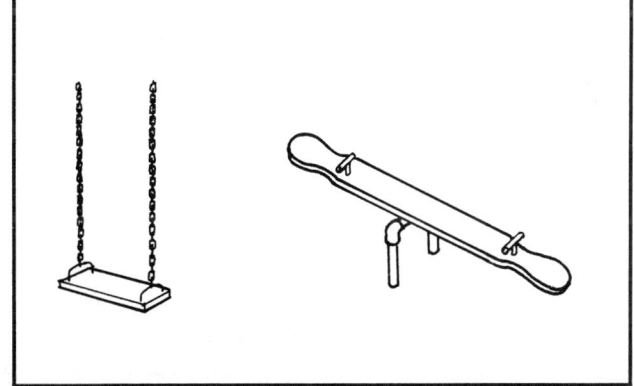

FOCUSING ON IMPORTANT FEATURES

Take a Look!

Name _____

Use these picture pairs to talk about differences.

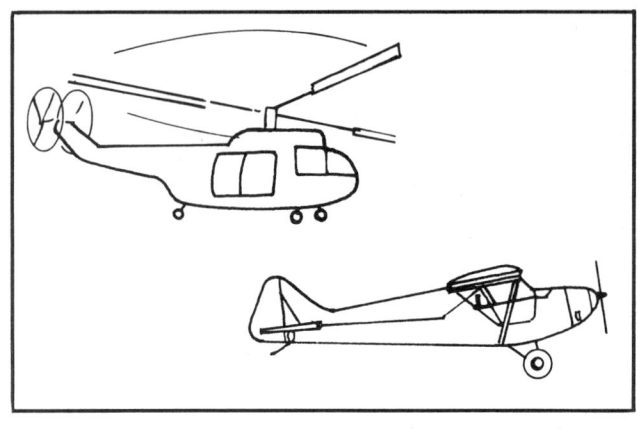

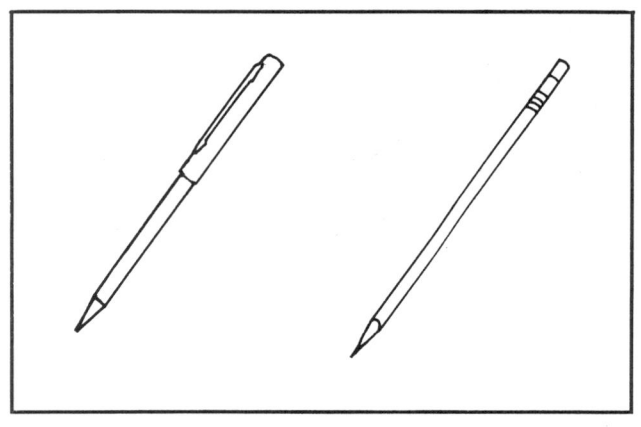

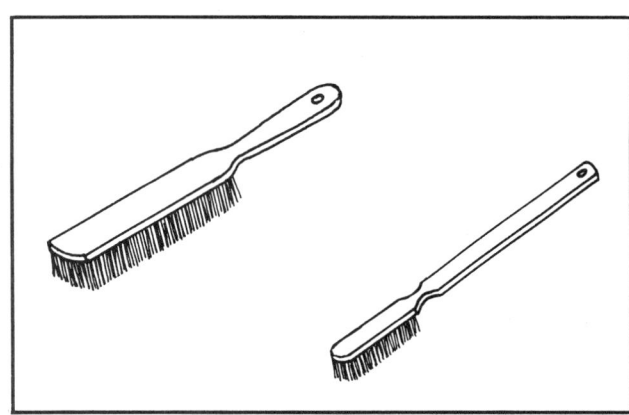
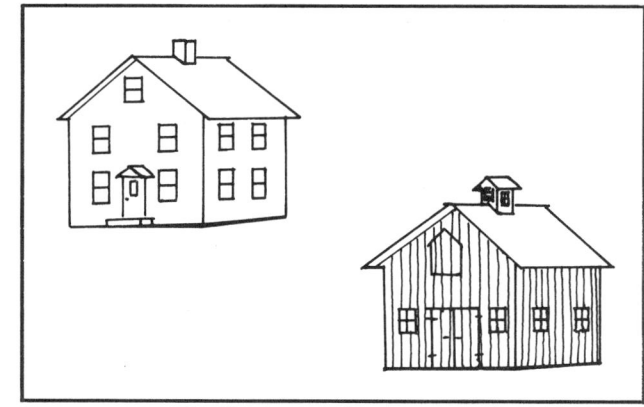
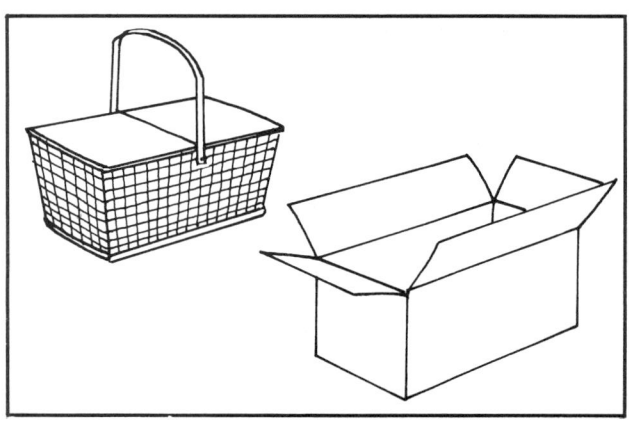

Tell the Difference

Name _____

Use these picture pairs to talk about differences.

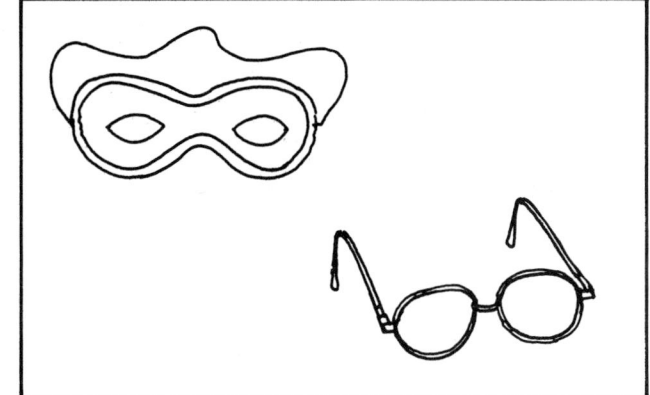
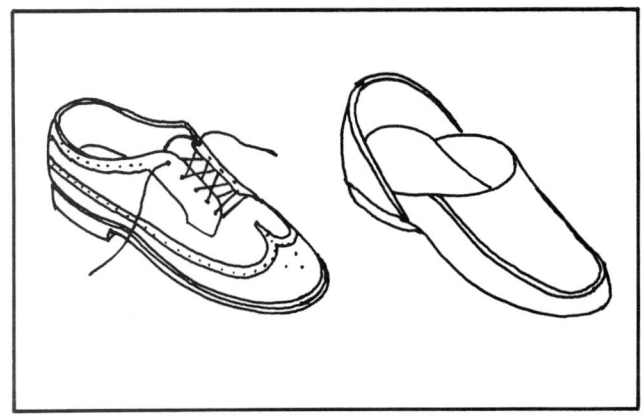
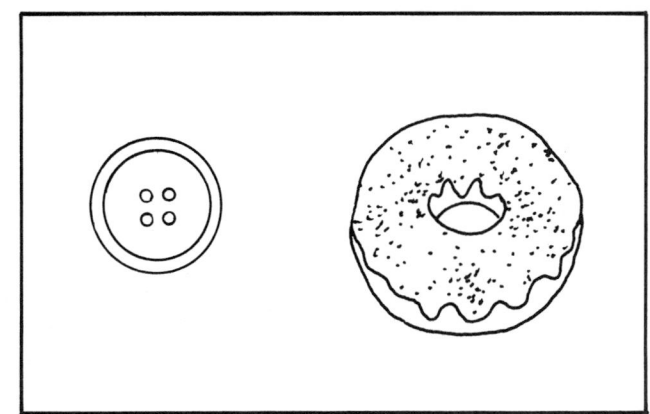

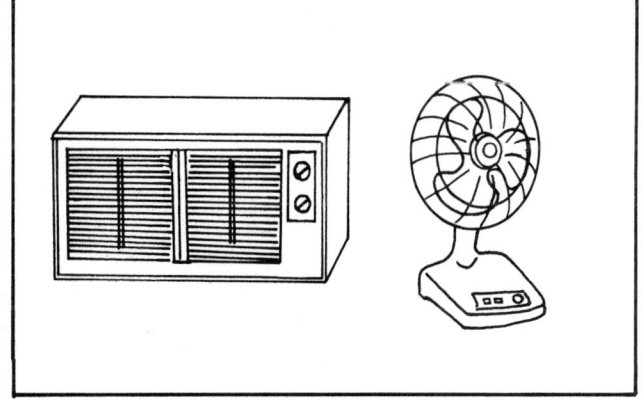

FOCUSING ON IMPORTANT FEATURES

Think about Differences

Name _____

Use these picture pairs to talk about differences.

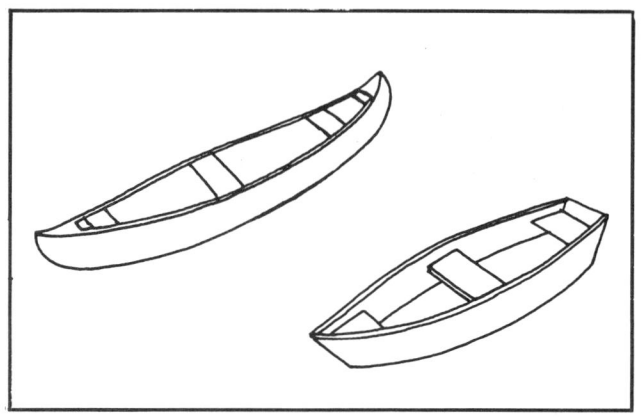

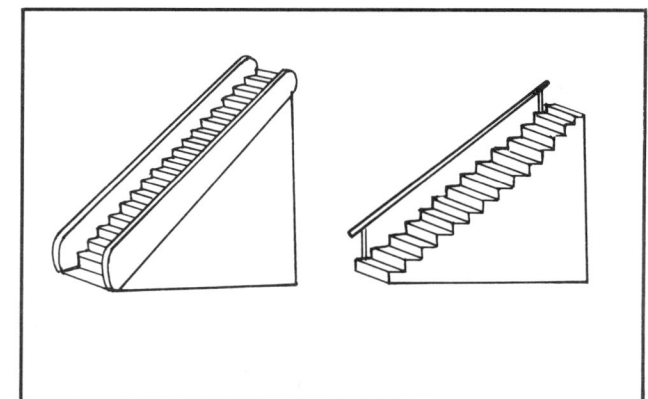

Level One Barrier Activities

These initial barrier activities are a fun, challenging way to demonstrate the need for effective communication. The listener has a limited number of items to choose from, yet the speaker must use specific descriptions to avoid confusion. For example, when describing the hat chosen for the clown, it is not sufficient to say "the hat with the stripes," since two hats have stripes. The speaker must also describe another discriminating feature, such as shape, in order for the listener to make the correct choice.

In addition, these barrier games teach students to request clarification when not enough information is presented. Too often, language-impaired students respond before they have all the necessary information. They tend to guess until the correct choice is discovered instead of asking for more information.

Practice with these barrier activities also helps students learn to evaluate the validity of the information received. The students learn that if the speaker describes an item incorrectly, the listener responds, "I don't have a _____ on my paper." Then, both the speaker and the listener are forced to use more descriptive language so that the item in question can be identified. A typical exchange follows:

> Speaker: It's the one with the things on his body.
> Listener: They all have something on their bodies!
> Speaker: I mean the lines.
> Listener: None of them has straight lines.
> Speaker: I mean curvy lines, like feathers.
> Listener: One set or two sets of feathers?
> Speaker: One set.
> Listener: I know which one it is now!

Instructions

Choose one of the Level One Barrier Activities on pages 90 through 101. Make copies of the picture outline and the associated features. Give one picture set to each student and place a barrier between them.

Step 1: Describe each chosen feature for the students to circle. Once the students have learned this task, proceed to Step 2.

Step 2: Have one student circle his choice of features and describe them for the other students to circle. Then, each student completes the picture with the features he circled.

For added variety, the speaker may also describe additional features (e.g., hair, nose, etc.) to enhance the picture.

After the picture descriptions, take away the barrier and compare pictures. Discuss possible reasons for any discrepancies.

Design a Clown

Name _____

Design a clown by choosing features from page 91.

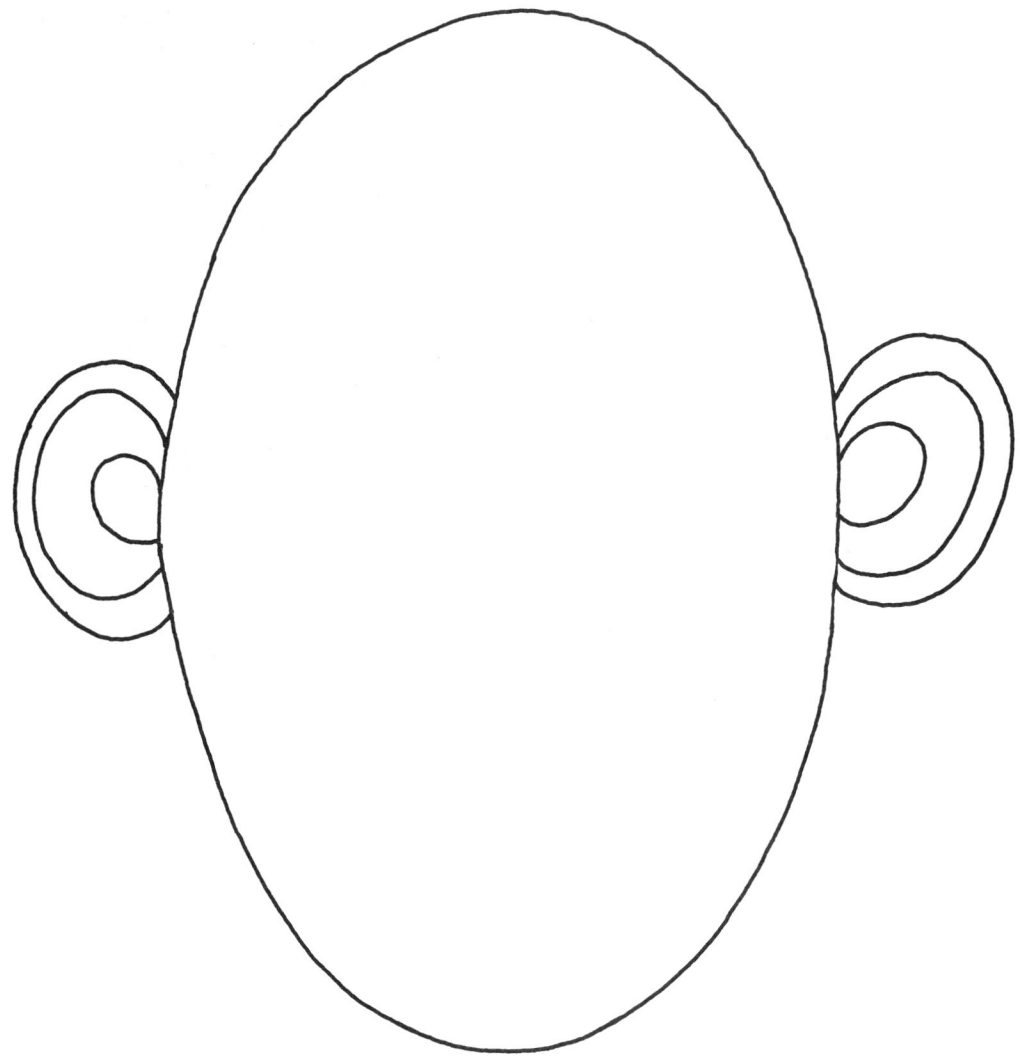

Design a Clown, continued

Name _____

Use these fun features to make a clown on page 90.

LEVEL ONE BARRIER ACTIVITIES   Copyright © 1987 LinguiSystems, Inc.

Design a House

Name _____

Design a house by choosing from the windows, doors, flower boxes, and chimneys on page 93.

LEVEL ONE BARRIER ACTIVITIES

Copyright © 1987 LinguiSystems, Inc.

Design a House, continued

Name _____

Use these pictures to make a house on page 92.

Chimneys	Windows

Flower Boxes	Doors

LEVEL ONE BARRIER ACTIVITIES

Design a Creature

Name _____

Design a creature by choosing features from page 95.

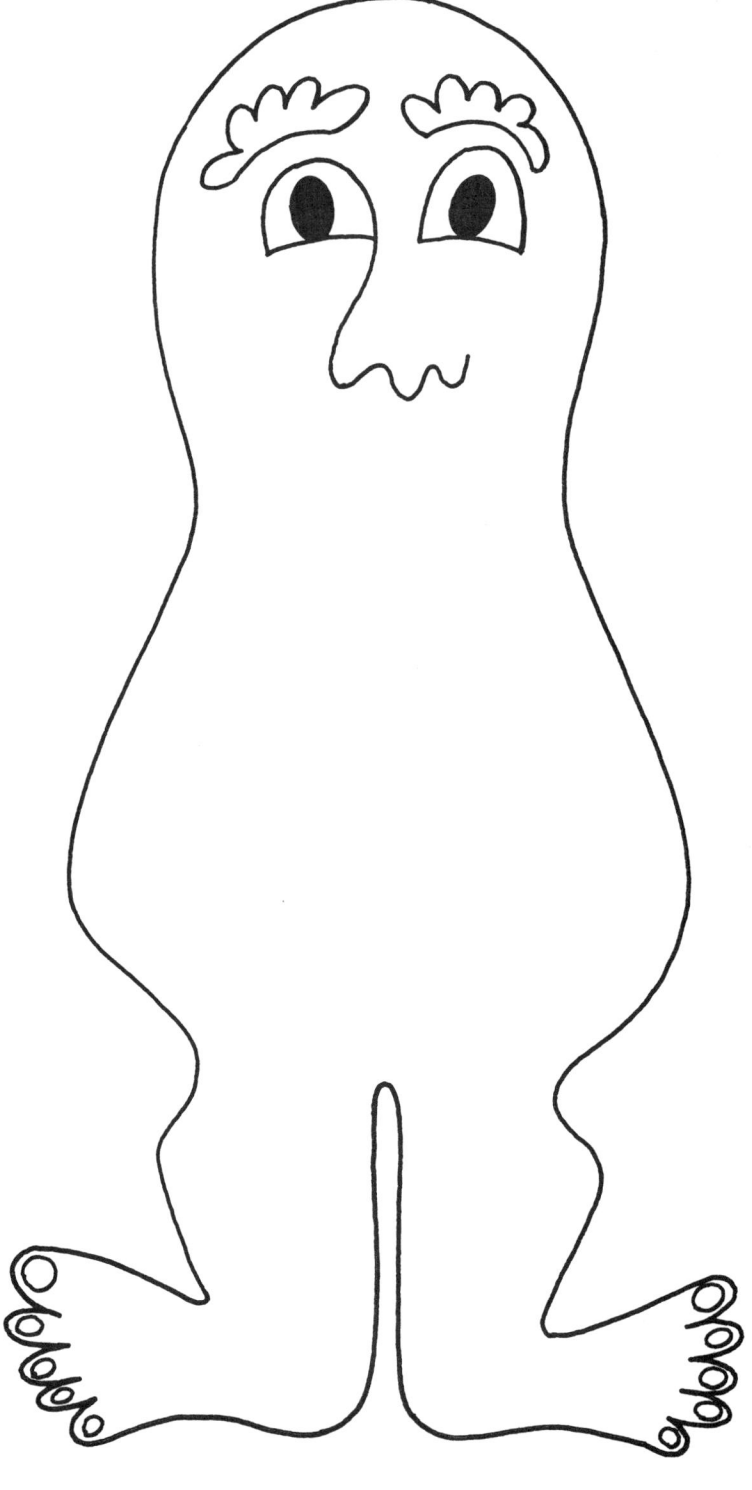

LEVEL ONE BARRIER ACTIVITIES
94
Copyright © 1987 LinguiSystems, Inc.

Design a Creature, continued   Name _____

Use these fun features to make a creature on page 94.

Horns	Arms

Tails	Mouths

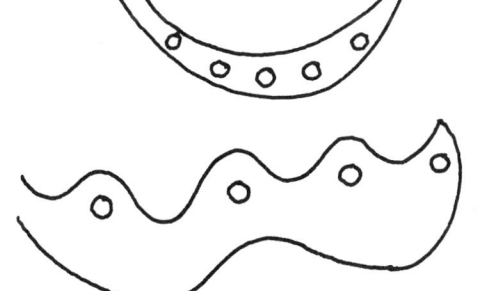
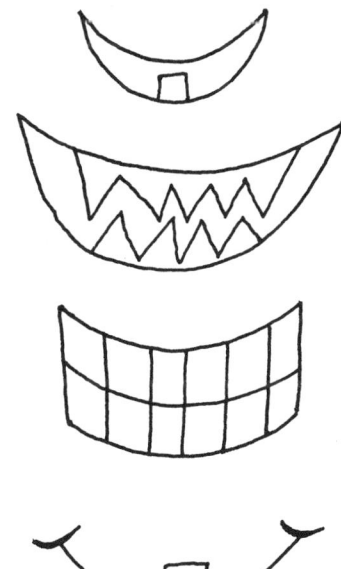

Design a Shirt

Name _____

Design a shirt by choosing from the sleeves, collars, pockets, and buttons on page 97.

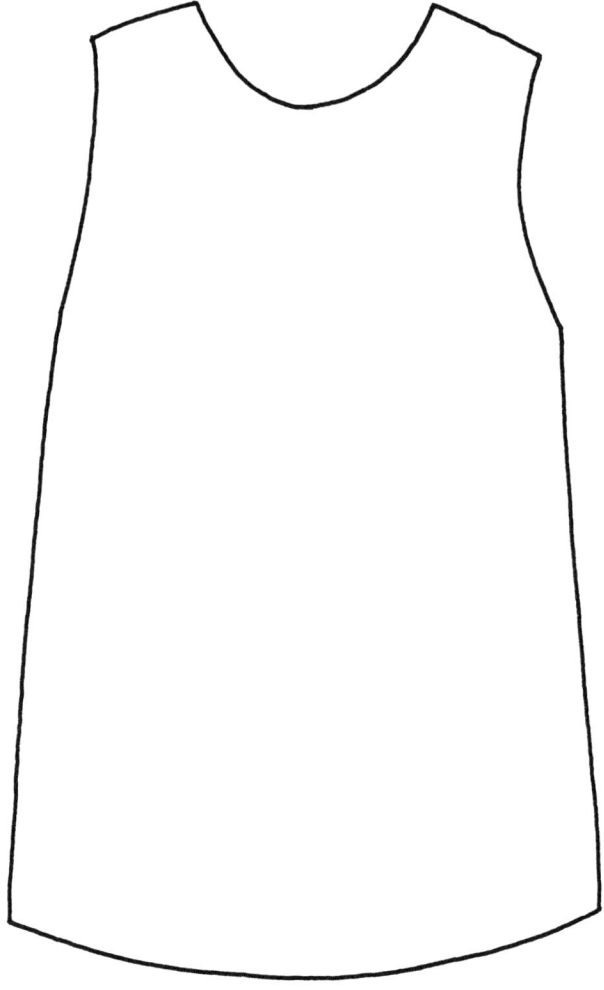

LEVEL ONE BARRIER ACTIVITIES

Design a Shirt, continued

Name _____

Use these pictures to make a shirt on page 96.

Collars

Buttons

Sleeves

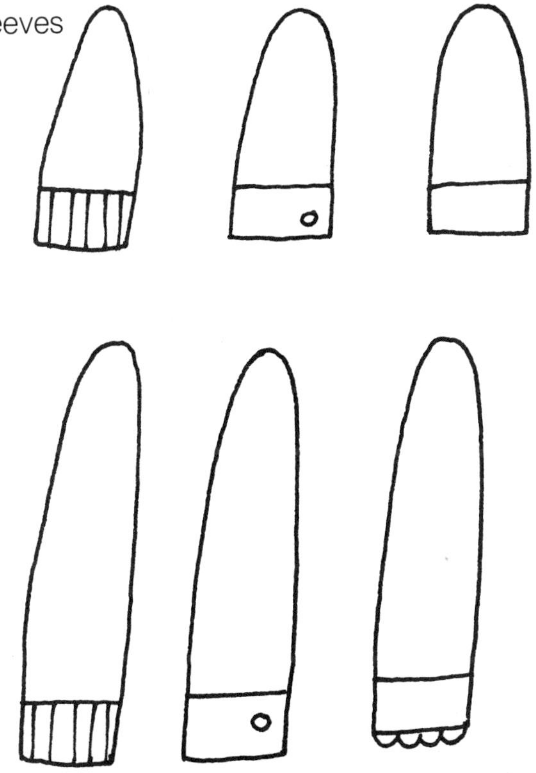

Pockets

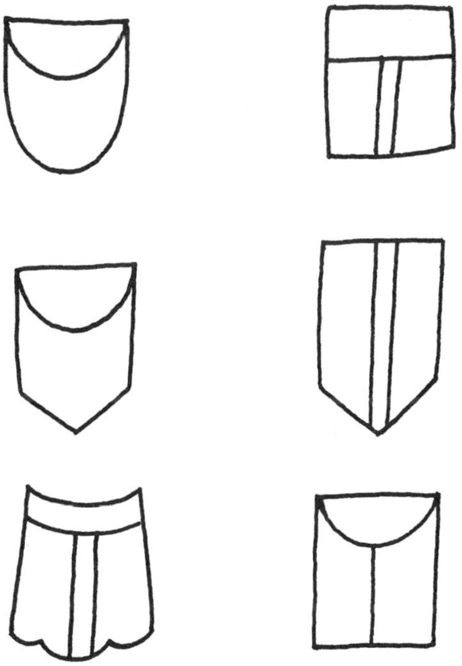

LEVEL ONE BARRIER ACTIVITIES

Design a Fish

Name _____

Design a fish by choosing features from page 99.

LEVEL ONE BARRIER ACTIVITIES 98 Copyright © 1987 LinguiSystems, Inc.

Design a Fish, continued

Name _____

Use these features to make a fish on page 98.

Eyes	Jaws

Scales	Tails

LEVEL ONE BARRIER ACTIVITIES

Design a Robot Warrior

Name _____

Design a robot warrior by choosing features from page 101.

LEVEL ONE BARRIER ACTIVITIES 100 Copyright © 1987 LinguiSystems, Inc.

Design a Robot Warrior, continued   Name _____

Use these features to make a robot warrior on page 100.

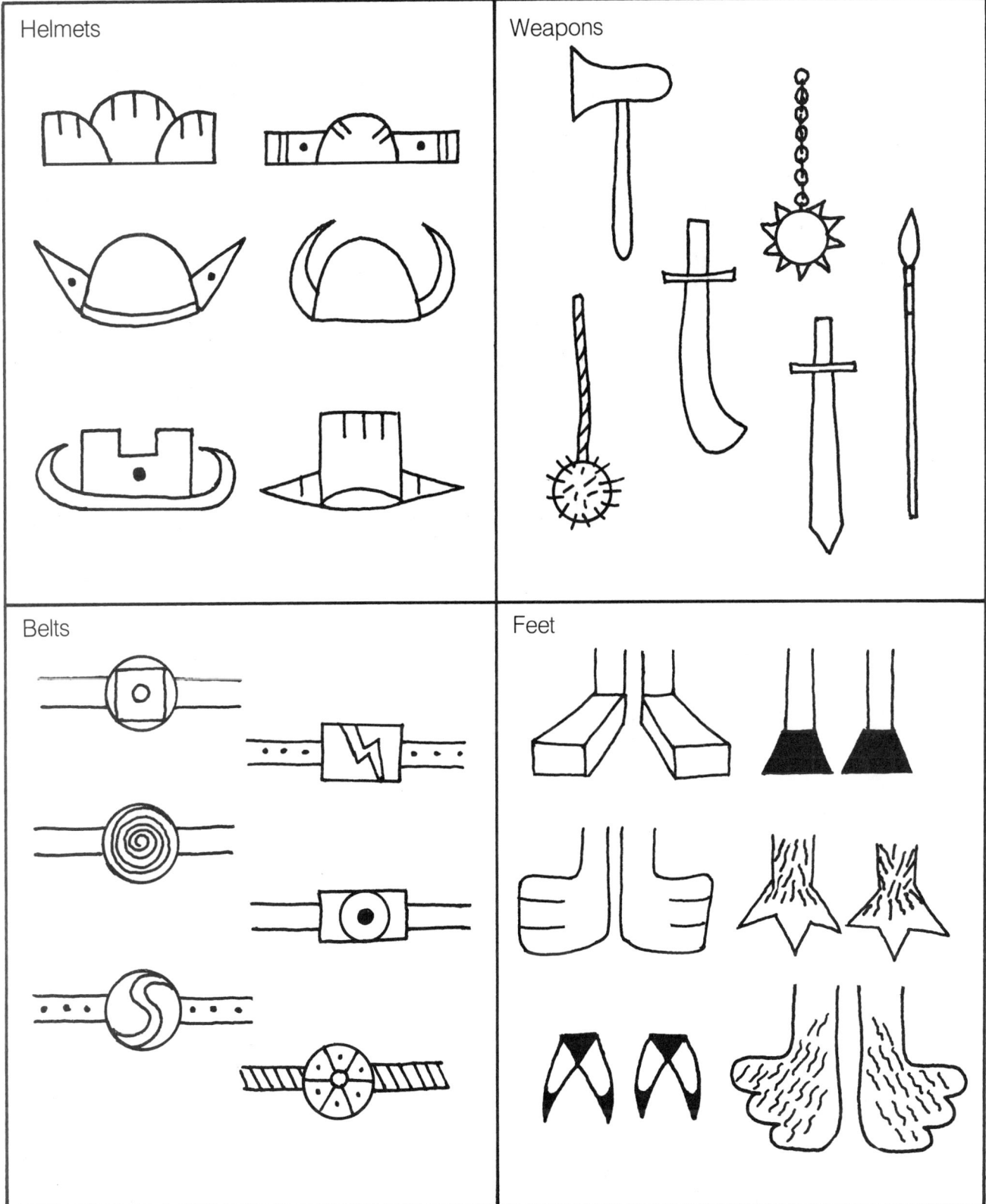

LEVEL ONE BARRIER ACTIVITIES

Level Two Barrier Activities

These intermediate barrier activities add variety and interest to the barrier task as the students attempt to replicate an original picture. These barrier activities are harder than the preceding ones because the students need to communicate not only which items are necessary, but their location as well.

For many students, manipulating pieces according to oral instructions is easier than drawing the design, as in Level Three. Level Two activities are also easier than the activities in Level Three from a correction standpoint, because when checking for accuracy, a student need only reposition an item rather than erase and start over.

Many art projects and classroom listening activities require the skills learned in Level Two Barrier Activities. Mastery of these activities leads to improved listening and language skills.

Instructions

Choose one of the activity pictures and the associated pictures on pages 103 through 110.

Step 1: Give one student the completed picture or have him arrange the pieces on the background scene. Have him tell the other students how to put the pieces together to form the desired picture.

Step 2: Distribute different parts of one picture to each student. Display the original picture, and instruct the students to work together to complete the picture. While the students work together, comment on the effectiveness of each student's language.

Take a Trip

Name _____

Use this page with the pictures from page 104 for fun as you listen or describe.

LEVEL TWO BARRIER ACTIVITIES — Copyright © 1987 LinguiSystems, Inc.

Take a Trip, continued

Name _____

Cut out these pictures. Use the pictures with the background scene for fun as you listen or describe.

LEVEL TWO BARRIER ACTIVITIES

At the Beach

Name _____

Use this page with the pictures from page 106 for fun as you listen or describe.

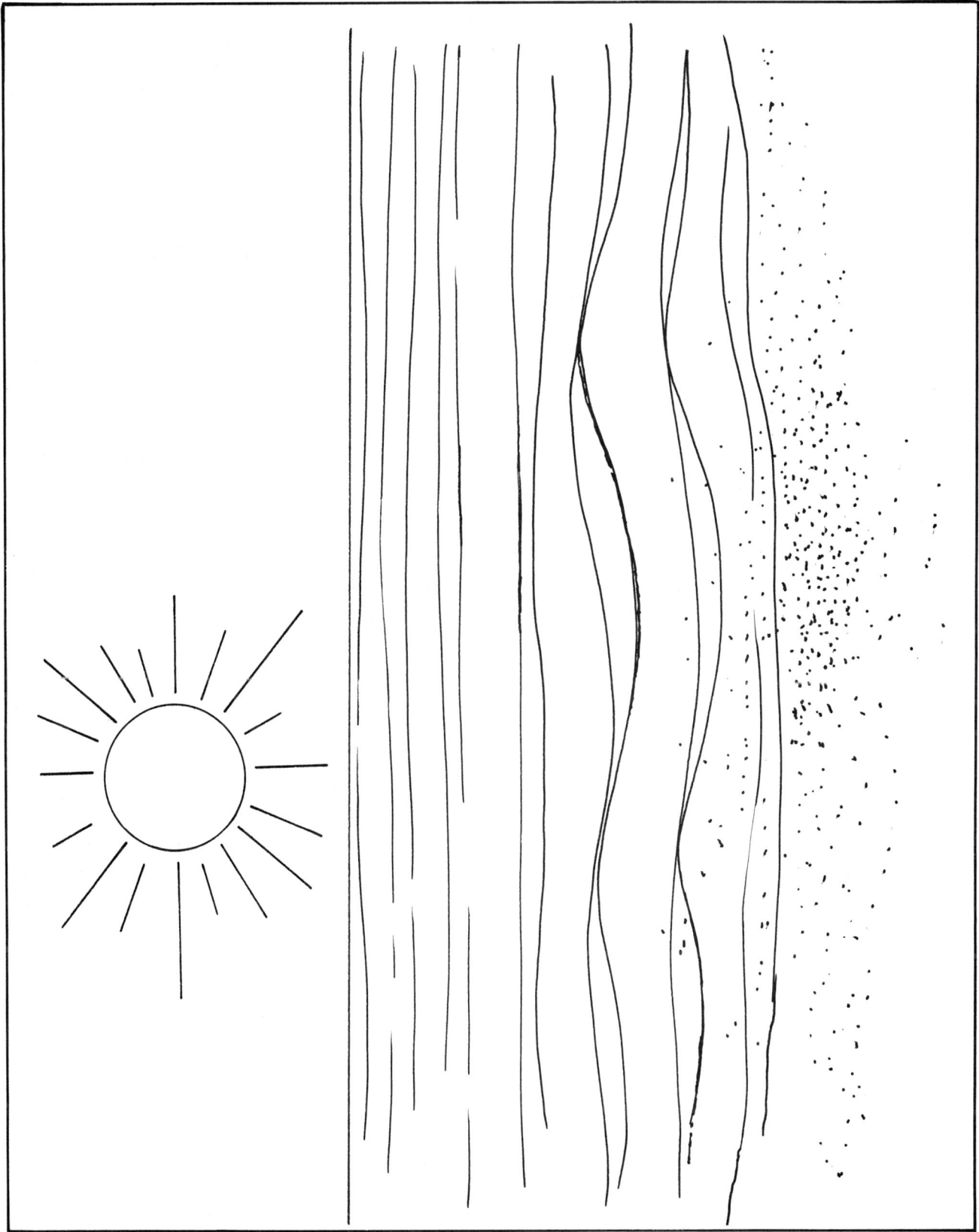

LEVEL TWO BARRIER ACTIVITIES

Copyright © 1987 LinguiSystems, Inc.

At the Beach, continued

Name _____

Cut out these pictures. Use the pictures with the background scene for fun as you listen or describe.

LEVEL TWO BARRIER ACTIVITIES

Winter Sledding Fun   Name _____

Use this page with the pictures from page 108 for fun as you listen or describe.

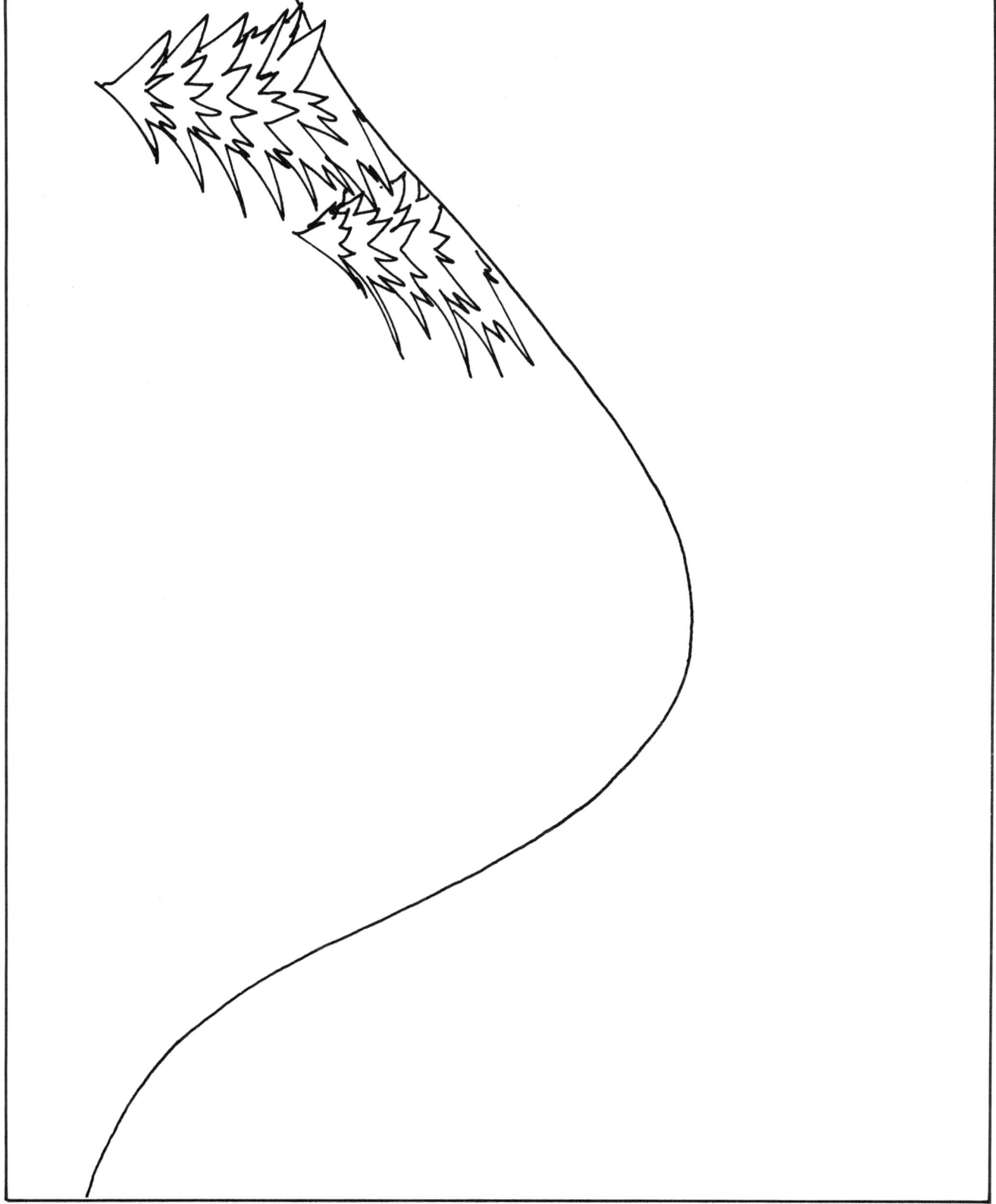

LEVEL TWO BARRIER ACTIVITIES

Winter Sledding Fun, continued   Name _____

Cut out these pictures. Use the pictures with the background scene for fun as you listen or describe.

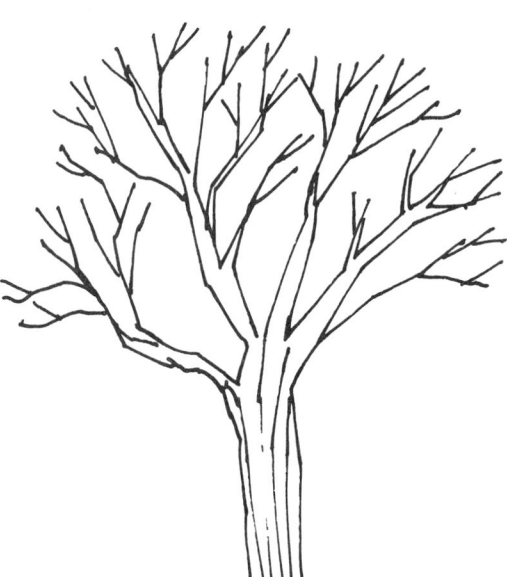

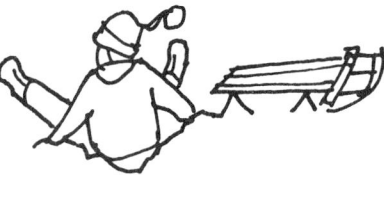

On My Block

Name _____

Use this page with the pictures from page 110 for fun as you listen or describe.

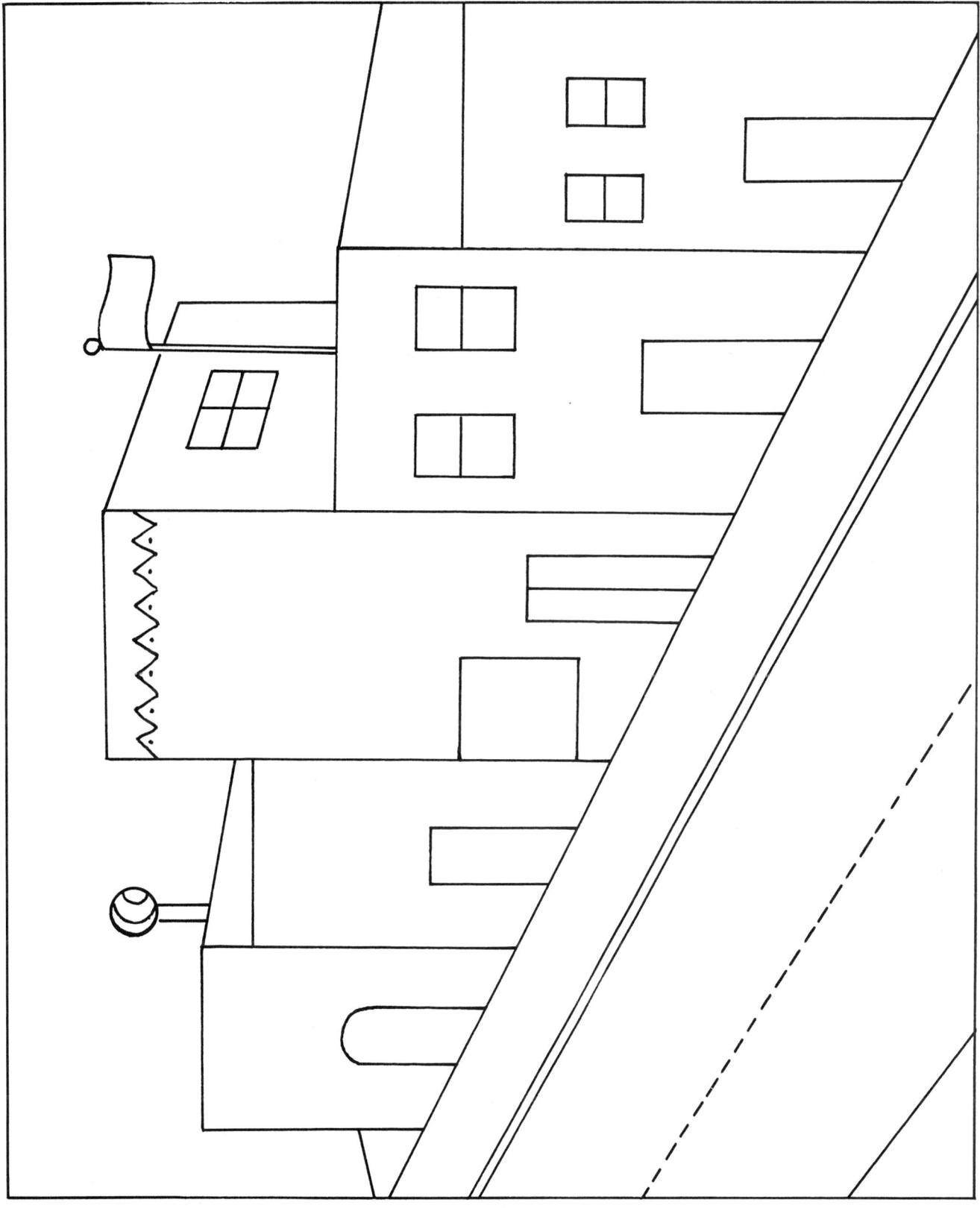

LEVEL TWO BARRIER ACTIVITIES

On My Block, continued

Name _____

Cut out these pictures. Use the pictures with the background scene for fun as you listen or describe.

LEVEL TWO BARRIER ACTIVITIES   110   Copyright © 1987 LinguiSystems, Inc.

Level Three Barrier Activities

The task of communicating is considerably more difficult within the framework of these barrier activities. The speaker adds features to a simple outline without the benefit of any example features and then describes his original picture to the listener. The listener completes his outline according to the speaker's instructions. The resulting picture may not be identical, but the number, shape, and positioning of items should be similar. How surprised some students are when the finished products are displayed and there are significant differences!

Instructions

In this unit, the speaker draws a feature on the blank outline. Then, he describes the feature and its placement to the listeners. The listeners draw the features and locate them as described. Record or transcribe the description process. Help the students learn to recognize where and why the communication failed by reviewing the descriptions after the pictures are completed.

Some suggested features for each activity are listed below.

Decorate a Christmas Tree, page 112

- Christmas balls
- garlands
- ornaments
- stockings
- tree-top decorations

Add a Hat, page 113

- brim
- earrings
- feathers
- ribbons
- shape of hat
- stars
- veil

Draw a Dinosaur, page 114

- claws
- eyes
- horns
- scales
- spikes
- teeth
- toenails

Draw a Dog, page 115

- collar
- ears
- eyes
- leash
- mouth
- nose
- spots
- tail
- teeth
- tongue

Decorate a Hot Air Balloon, page 116

- hearts
- letters
- stripes
- zigzags

Add a Picture, page 117

- farm
- flowers
- house
- people

Decorate a Birthday Cake, page 118

- candles
- flowers
- greetings
- holiday decorations

Choose one of the activity pictures on pages 112 through 118.

Step 1: Play the part of the speaker by adding features and describing them for the students to draw.

Step 2: Add features to the picture and have a student describe them for the other students to draw.

Step 3: Have one student add features to the outline and describe them for the other students to draw.

Decorate a Christmas Tree

Name _____

Use this fun page as you listen or describe.

LEVEL THREE BARRIER ACTIVITIES

Add a Hat

Name _____

Use this fun page as you listen or describe.

LEVEL THREE BARRIER ACTIVITIES   113   Copyright © 1987 LinguiSystems, Inc.

Draw a Dinosaur

Name _____

Use this fun page as you listen or describe.

LEVEL THREE BARRIER ACTIVITIES

Draw a Dog

Name _____

Use this fun page as you listen or describe.

LEVEL THREE BARRIER ACTIVITIES

Decorate a Hot Air Balloon

Name _____

Use this fun page as you listen or describe.

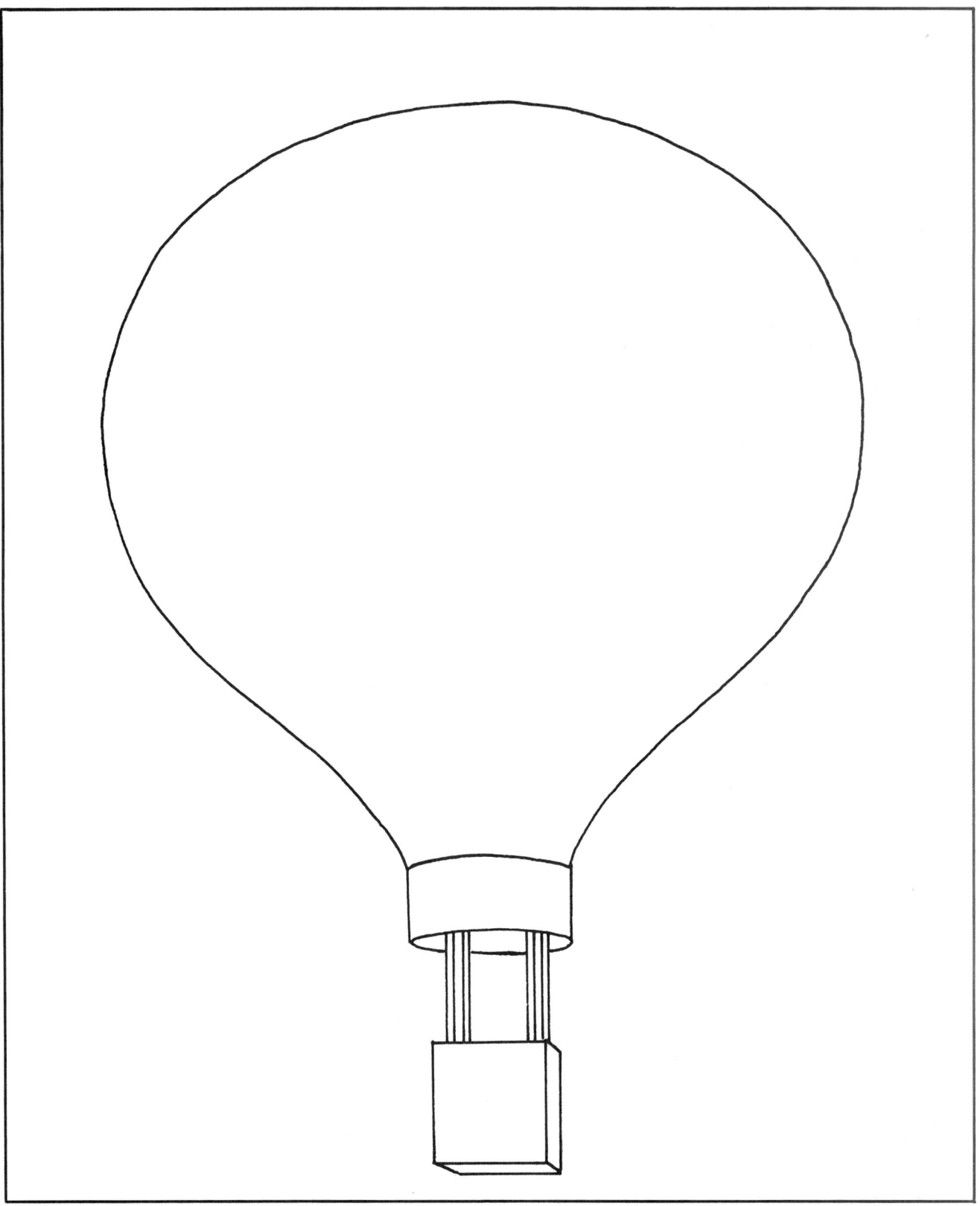

LEVEL THREE BARRIER ACTIVITIES

Add a Picture Name _____

Use this fun page as you listen or describe.

TITLE:
ARTIST:

LEVEL THREE BARRIER ACTIVITIES

Decorate a Birthday Cake

Name _____

Use this fun page as you listen or describe.

LEVEL THREE BARRIER ACTIVITIES 118 Copyright © 1987 LinguiSystems, Inc.

Focusing on Discriminating Features

The activities in this unit teach the student to identify the discriminating features among similar objects. Students are expected to perform such tasks in their daily living. For example, a student may be asked to request a specific doughnut from a large assortment of trays in a bakery. A response of "the chocolate one" is insufficient when there are many varieties of chocolate doughnuts. The student who responds "the one with the stuff on top" is also failing to communicate his choice effectively. The language-impaired student may frequently resort to gesturing in the direction of his choice and say "that one." The failure to communicate effectively occurs because the student does not recognize and name the discriminating feature of his choice when compared to the other doughnuts.

Acquisition of this skill is important because academic learning requires discrimination. For example, in phonics, students must recognize the difference between *b* and *d*, and *was* and *saw*. In science, students learn the difference between a crocodile and an alligator. In social studies, they must discriminate between a city and a town. These exercises will help students learn to focus on discrete differences of similar items.

Instructions

This unit allows much flexibility in teaching effective communication skills, and emphasizes the need to request more information. To demonstrate poor communication skills, assume the role of the speaker. Have each student place a copy of one of the activity sheets behind a barrier. For example, using the Teddy Bear activity sheet, say, "This bear has a vest. Which one is it?" Because all the teddy bears have vests, the students must request more information before they can identify the correct bear. Continue to give non-discriminating clues, pointing out that although the information is correct, the clues do not impart enough new information to enable a correct choice.

On the other hand, when teaching the concept of discriminating features, give the students only one clue. Have them search for the one bear with that particular feature. For example, "This teddy bear has black ears."

When first exposed to this task, many language-impaired students do not know how to organize the incoming information to find the correct answer. These same students may have difficulty with reading in the classroom. They may respond correctly to comprehension questions about literal information in the stories but have difficulty projecting the outcome, deducing the answer, and fully comprehending implied ideas. Practice with these discrete discrimination tasks helps students learn how to use complementing bits of information to deduce the correct answer.

For additional practice and reinforcement of these skills, use the Picture Pair Discrimination activities, pages 83 through 88.

Teddy Bears 1

Step 1: Discuss the differences and similarities among the bears on page 121. Ask questions such as:

> Which bears have vests?
> Which bears have little eyes?
> Which bears are little?
> Which bears are big?
> Which bears have glasses?
> Which bears have freckles?
> Which bears have striped vests?   (polka dot vests, checkered vests)
> What do all the bears have?
> What does only one bear have?
> What do some bears have, but not the other bears?

Step 2: Place a barrier between the students. Give clues and have the students ask for more information as needed. First, give non-discriminating clues, such as "This bear is wearing glasses." Then, the students must say, "There are two bears wearing glasses." Have them suggest what kind of clue would help. For example, "What kind of vest is he wearing?" Or, if this task is too difficult, have them simply say that they need more information. Proceed with the activity until one of the students has enough information to identify the correct bear.

> Variation: Give discriminating clues, such as "This bear is wearing a bow tie," or "This little bear has a striped vest."

Step 3: Place a barrier between the students. Have one student give clues to the other students. Choose one of these formats:

> a. give any kind of clue (non-discriminating or discriminating),
> b. give non-discriminating clues, or
> c. give as few discriminating clues as possible.

Then, have the students switch speaker and listener roles and repeat the activity with these pictures or similar stimulus pictures (e.g., Which Gift Box, page 123).

Which Teddy Bear?

Name _____

Talk about how these bears are alike and different.

A.

B.

C.

D.

E.

F.

FOCUSING ON DISCRIMINATING FEATURES

Gift Boxes 1

Step 1: Discuss the differences and similarities among the gift boxes on page 123. Ask questions such as:

    Which boxes are wrapped with plain paper?
    Which boxes are wrapped with striped paper? (horizontally striped, vertically striped, diagonally striped)
    Which boxes have a solid ribbon? (striped ribbon)
    Which boxes have a curly bow? (untied bow, solid, tied bow)
    Which boxes have a lid?
    What do all the boxes have?
    What does only one box have?
    What do some boxes have, but not the other boxes?

Step 2: Place a barrier between the students. Give clues and have the students ask for more information as needed. First, give non-discriminating clues, such as "This box has a bow." Then, the students must say, "All the boxes have a bow." Have them suggest what kind of clue would help. For example, "What kind of bow does it have?" Or, if this task is too difficult, have them simply say that they need more information. Proceed with the activity until one of the students has enough information to identify the target gift box.

Variation: Give discriminating clues, such as "This gift box is small."

Step 3: Place a barrier between the students. Have one student give clues to the other students. Choose one of the following formats:

    a. give any kind of clue (non-discriminating or discriminating),
    b. give non-discriminating clues, or
    c. give as few discriminating clues as possible.

Then, have the students switch speaker and listener roles and repeat the activity with these pictures or similar stimulus pictures (e.g., Which Owl, page 125).

Which Gift Box?

Name _____

Talk about how these gift boxes are alike and different.

A.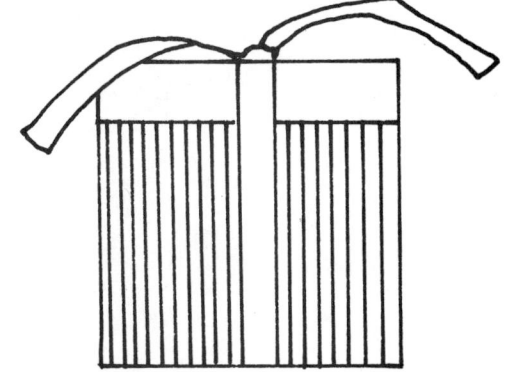

B.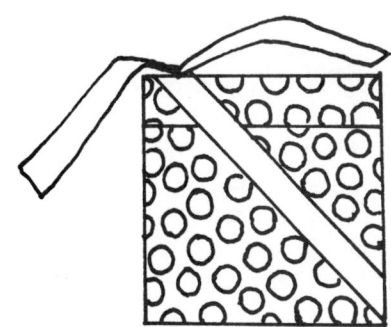

C.

D.

E.

F.

FOCUSING ON DISCRIMINATING FEATURES

Owls 1

Step 1: Discuss the differences and similarities among the owls on page 125. Ask questions such as:

> Which owls have glasses?
> Which owls have black beaks?
> Which owls have black legs?
> Which owls have long legs?
> Which owl has pointed claws?
> Which owl is tall?
> Which owls have black ears?
> What do all the owls have?
> What does only one owl have?
> What do some owls have, but not the other owls?

Step 2: Place a barrier between the students. Give clues and have the students ask for more information, as needed. First, give non-discriminating clues, such as "This owl has black legs." Then, the students must say, "There are two owls with black legs." Have them suggest what kind of clue would help. For example, "Is the owl tall or short?" Or, if this task is too difficult, have them simply say that they need more information. Proceed with the activity until one of the students has enough information to identify the correct owl.

Variation: Give discriminating clues, such as "This owl has pointed, sharp claws."

Step 3: Place a barrier between the students. Have one student give clues to the other student. Choose one of the following formats:

a. give any kind of clue (non-discriminating or discriminating),
b. give non-discriminating clues, or
c. give as few discriminating clues as possible.

Then, have the students switch speaker and listener roles and repeat the activity with these pictures or similar stimulus pictures (e.g., Which Ice Cream Cone, page 127).

Which Owl?

Name _____

Talk about how these owls are alike and different.

A.

B.

C.

D.

E.

F.

Ice Cream Cones 1

Step 1: Discuss the differences and similarities among the ice cream cones on page 127. Ask questions such as:

> Which ice cream cones have a triangular shape? (flat bottom)
> Which cones have swirled ice cream? (big, round scoops; flat scoops)
> Which cones have chocolate ice cream? (vanilla)
> Which cones have horizontal lines? (vertical lines; diagonal lines)
> Which cones are chocolate?
> What do all of the ice cream cones have?
> What does only one ice cream cone have?
> What do some but not all of the cones have?

Step 2: Place a barrier between the students. Give clues and have the students ask for more information, as needed. First, give non-discriminating clues, such as "This ice cream cone has lines on it." Then, the students must say, "There are six ice cream cones with lines on them." Have them suggest what kind of clue would help. For example, "Is the ice cream cone chocolate?" Or, if this task is too difficult, have them simply say that they need more information. Proceed with the activity until one of the students has enough information to identify the correct ice cream cone.

Variation: Give discriminating clues, such as "This ice cream cone has a cherry on top."

Step 3: Place a barrier between the students. Have one student give clues to the other students. Choose one of the following formats:

a. give any kind of clue (non-discriminating or discriminating),
b. give non-discriminating clues, or
c. give as few discriminating clues as possible.

Then, have the students switch speaker and listener roles and repeat the activity with these pictures or similar stimulus pictures (e.g., Which Room, page 129).

Which Ice Cream Cone?

Name _____

Talk about how these ice cream cones are alike and different.

A.

B.

C.

D.

E.

F.

FOCUSING ON DISCRIMINATING FEATURES

Rooms in a House 1

Step 1: Discuss the differences and similarities among the rooms on page 129. Ask questions such as:

> Which rooms have beds?
> Which rooms have tables?
> Which rooms have rugs?
> Which rooms have a television set?
> Which rooms have a bathtub?
> Which bedroom has pictures on the wall?
> What do all the rooms have?
> What does only one room have?
> What do some of the rooms have, but not the other rooms?

Step 2: Place a barrier between the students. Give clues and have the students ask for more information, as needed. First, give non-discriminating clues, such as "This room has a window." Then, the students must say, "There are four rooms with windows." Have them suggest what kind of clue would help. For example, "Does the room have a television set?" Or, if this task is too difficult, have them simply say that they need more information. Proceed with the activity until one of the students has enough information to identify the correct room.

Variation: Give discriminating clues, such as "This bathroom has a washer and dryer."

Step 3: Place a barrier between the students. Have one student give clues to the other students. Choose one of the following formats:

  a. give any kind of clue (non-discriminating or discriminating),
  b. give non-discriminating clues, or
  c. give as few discriminating clues as possible.

Then, have the students switch speaker and listener roles and repeat the activity with these pictures or similar stimulus pictures (e.g., Which Teddy Bear, page 121).

Which Room?

Name _____

Talk about how these rooms are alike and different.

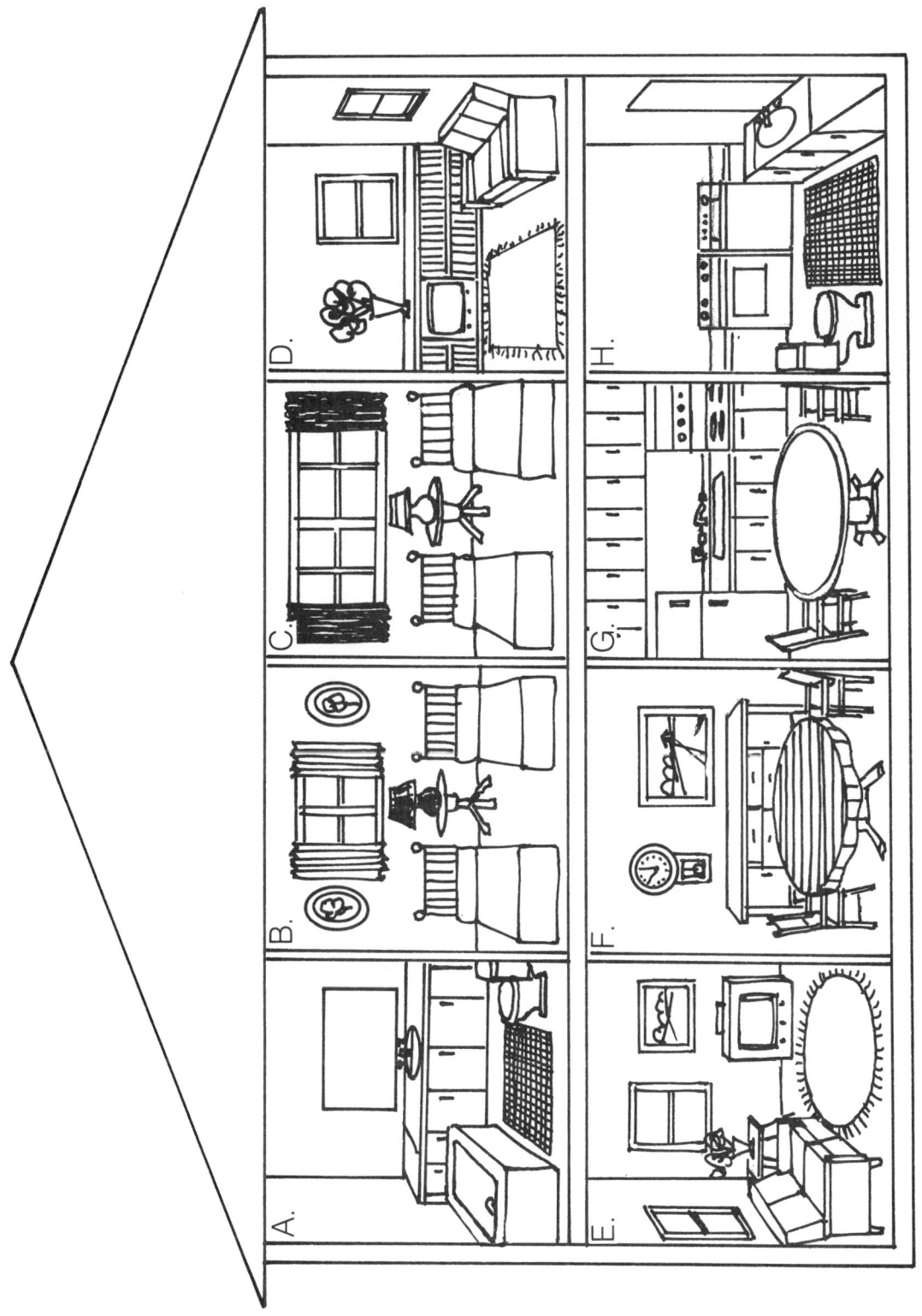

FOCUSING ON DISCRIMINATING FEATURES

Copyright © 1987 LinguiSystems, Inc.

Exclusion

Once the student has mastered the technique of focusing on discriminating features, introduce the concept of exclusion. While students usually learn quickly how to use the process of elimination to find an answer, negative statements make the task more difficult. Decoding and acting upon the negative statements involves a two-step process. First, the student must recognize the target attribute. Then, he must remember to avoid it. Thus, in order to succeed on such a task, the student learns that a statement such as "This bear does not have a striped vest" means that he eliminates or crosses out all bears wearing striped vests. This ability to exclude information appropriately is essential for students to learn if they are to respond accurately to qualified commands and instructions, such as "Any student who does not finish his assignment will miss recess."

Teddy Bears 2

Give all students an identical copy of Which Teddy Bear, page 121, and place a barrier between them. Read the negative statements below and have the students identify the correct bear. When the students have mastered the listening task, have each of them create their own negative statements.

Clues *Answers*

1. This bear is not wearing glasses.
2. His vest is not checkered.
3. He is not small.
4. He does not have black ears.

B.

1. This bear does not have dots on his vest.
2. He is not wearing glasses.
3. He is not big.
4. He does not have a half-circle on his face.

C.

1. This bear is not small.
2. He does not have a tie.
3. He does not have dots on his vest.
4. He does not have white ears.

E.

1. This bear does not have black ears.
2. He does not have dots on his vest.
3. He does not have a half-circle on his face.
4. He is not small.

D.

1. This bear does not have glasses.
2. He does not have dots on his vest.
3. He does not have black ears.
4. He does not have stripes on his vest.

A.

1. This bear is not small.
2. He does not have black ears.
3. He does not have checks on his vest.
4. He does not have stitches on his hands and feet.

F.

EXCLUSION

Gift Boxes 2

Give all students an identical copy of Which Gift Box, page 123, and place a barrier between them. Read the negative statements below and have the students identify the correct gift box. When the students have mastered the listening task, have each of them create their own negative statements.

Clues

Answers

1. This gift box is not wrapped in plain paper.
2. It does not have paper with circles on it.
3. It does not have a lid.
4. It is not wrapped in paper with diagonal stripes on it.

1. This gift box does not have a curly ribbon.
2. It does not have a diagonal ribbon.
3. It does not have a lid.
4. It is not wrapped in paper with horizontal stripes.

1. This gift box does not have a curly ribbon.
2. It is not wrapped in paper with diagonal stripes.
3. It does not have a plain bow.
4. It does not have a diagonal ribbon.

1. This gift box is not wrapped in plain paper.
2. It does not have a curly ribbon.
3. It does not have striped wrapping paper.

1. This gift box is not wrapped in striped paper.
2. It does not have an untied bow.
3. It is not wrapped in plain paper.

1. This gift box is not wrapped in paper with circles on it.
2. It does not have a plain bow.
3. It does not have an untied bow.

EXCLUSION

Owls 2

Give all students an identical copy of Which Owl, page 125, and place a barrier between them. Read the negative statements below and have the students identify the correct owl. When the students have mastered the listening task, have each of them create their own negative statements.

Clues *Answers*

1. This owl does not wear glasses.
2. It does not have long legs.
3. It does not have white ears.
4. It does not have black feet.

F.

1. This owl does not have long legs.
2. It does not have black feet.
3. It does not wear glasses.
4. It does not have black ears.

C.

1. This owl does not have sharp claws.
2. Its ears are not all white.
3. It does not wear glasses.
4. It does not have a black beak.

D.

1. This owl does not have long legs.
2. It does not have black feet.
3. It doesn't have all white ears.
4. It does not have semi-circles for eyes.

B.

1. This owl does not have a white beak.
2. It does not have black feet.
3. It does not have fluffy feathers around its eyes.
4. It does not have oval eyes.

E.

1. This owl does not have sharp, pointed claws.
2. It does not wear glasses.
3. It does not have long legs.
4. It does not have white legs.

A.

Ice Cream Cones 2

Give all students an identical copy of Which Ice Cream Cone, page 127, and place a barrier between them. Read the negative statements below and have the students identify the correct ice cream cone. When the students have mastered the listening task, have each of them create their own negative statements.

Clues *Answers*

A.

1. This ice cream cone does not have horizontal lines.
2. It is not dripping.
3. It does not have two scoops of ice cream.
4. It does not have a cherry on top.

F.

1. This ice cream cone is not swirled.
2. It does not have a cherry on top.
3. It does not have chocolate ice cream.

D.

1. This ice cream cone does not have a flat bottom.
2. It does not have vanilla ice cream.
3. It does not have swirled ice cream.

E.

1. This ice cream cone is not dripping.
2. It does not have horizontal or vertical lines.
3. It does not have chocolate ice cream.

C.

1. This ice cream cone does not have a cherry on top.
2. It does not have a chocolate cone.
3. It does not have chocolate ice cream.

B.

1. This ice cream cone does not have a triangular shaped cone.
2. It does not have diagonal lines.

EXCLUSION

Rooms in a House 2

Give all students an identical copy of Which Room, page 129, and place a barrier between them. Read the negative statements below and have the students identify the correct room. When the students have mastered the listening task, have each of them create their own negative statements.

Clues Answers

1. This room does not have a bed.
2. It does not have chairs.
3. It does not have a window.
4. It does not have a bathtub.

1. This room does not have a television set.
2. It does not have a throw rug.
3. It does not have a lamp.
4. It does not have a sink.

1. This room does not have a mirror.
2. It does not have a tablecloth.
3. It does not have a picture on the wall.
4. It does not have a window.

1. This room does not have a window.
2. It does not have chairs.
3. It does not have a washer and dryer.
4. It does not have a picture on the wall.

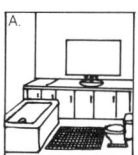

1. This room does not have a picture on the wall.
2. It does not have a washer and dryer.
3. It does not have a television set.
4. It does not have a sink.

1. This room does not have curtains.
2. It does not have a sink.
3. It does not have a table.
4. It does not have a picture on the wall.

1. This room does not have a television set.
2. It does not have a chair.
3. It does not have a sink.
4. It does not have black curtains.

1. This room does not have a tablecloth.
2. It does not have a rectangular throw rug.
3. It does not have a mirror on the wall.
4. It does not have a bare floor.

EXCLUSION

Additional Suggestions

Barrier Activities

It is relatively easy to acquire appropriate materials for barrier games. Keep identical sets of blocks, objects, and illustrations on hand. Many of the materials can be purchased at a variety store. Some materials and specific suggestions for using these materials are listed below.

1. *Colorforms sets which contain a background scene*   One student can arrange the individual pieces on the background and then instruct the others to place their figures in the same manner.

2. *Toy towns, circuses, or safari sets to punch out*   One student can arrange the individual pieces and then instruct the other students to place the pieces in the arrangement.

3. *Paper dolls with a variety of clothing*   One student selects an article of clothing and describes it so the others can choose the same piece for their dolls.

4. *Sets of Legos or interlocking blocks*   One student makes a certain geometric figure and then instructs the others to do the same.

5. *Tic-Tac-Toe grids*   Each player must describe where he chooses to put his X or O on the board as he plays Tic-Tac-Toe.

6. *Floor plans*   Each student can draw a floor plan of his home, town, or school. The speaker can then explain (1) how to get from one place to another, (2) how to arrange furniture in certain rooms, or (3) how to get from one section of town to another.

7. *Sets of different colored shapes*   Have one student make an arrangement of something familiar (e.g., a truck, bird, house, etc.), and then instruct the others how to make it. Ask the other students to name the finished product.

In these barrier activities, if it is initially too difficult for the students to alternate speaker and listener roles, play the speaker and direct the students in a listening activity.

Group Activities

1. *Feely Bag*   Fill a bag or a box with familiar items, especially those with different shapes and textures. The speaker reaches inside, picks an item, and describes its most important features by touch. Help the students evaluate the information value of the clues and try to guess what the item is. If appropriate, make the task more difficult by allowing the speaker to give only a single clue.

2. *Animal Identification*   Using small plastic animals, line up the animals which have a similar characteristic (e.g., all white, all big, all farm, all wild, or all spotted). Tell the students you have a certain animal in mind and they must guess the animal by listening to the clues, such as "It has legs." Remind the students to evaluate the clues and request more information if necessary. Become more specific in giving clues. Do not allow students to guess until they are absolutely certain of the answer.

   For students who have difficulty with this task, remove the animals which do not fit each clue, eventually leaving only the correct choice.

3. *Who Is It?*   Begin with "I'm thinking of a person in this room" and give non-informative clues, such as "This person has a head." Make subsequent clues more specific. Students must recognize when to request more information and cannot guess until certain of the correct answer.

4. *Fish Game* Use children's card games which involve matching. Instead of requesting the matching card by name, the students describe what the card looks like (e.g., "I need the girl with the lace on the bottom of her dress"). Act as the communicative guide, offering help when needed.

5. *Posters* Use photographs or posters of action scenes. Have the students go from general information to specific detail to describe the scene as outlined in the unit on scene descriptions.

6. *Categorization* Use small plastic animals, pictures of common objects, or small toys. Instruct the students to agree on the manner in which the objects should be grouped. For example, animals can be classified into big/small, farm/wild, hooves/paws, or plant/meat-eating. Then, ask the students to find a different way to regroup the same items.

7. *Instructions* Ask one student to explain an unfamiliar game to the other students. Coach the speaker in organizing the information (e.g., the objective of the game, roles of participants, sequence of rules, or clear referents), and encourage the listeners to ask for clarification if necessary.

8. *Association* Rule a 22" x 28" piece of posterboard into two-inch squares. Choose small pictures of associated items (e.g., comb/brush, bat/ball, etc.). One student places a pair anywhere on the board. Another student describes how to get from one picture to the other (e.g., "Go four squares north and two squares west"). The student who gives the correct instructions places the next pair of pictures on the board.

9. *Similes* For additional practice, have the students suggest multiple responses to complete similes. Since *Find Your Way with Words* concentrates on the visual area of perception, use similes in the other areas of hearing, touch, and taste, such as *quiet as a* _____ , *slippery as a* _____ , or *sweet as a* _____ .

Cut and Place

1. *Jack-O'-Lanterns* Put the materials to be used in the center of the table. Ask the students to offer suggestions as a group for the sequence of how to carve the pumpkin and which materials to use. Encourage descriptive language, turn-taking, and so forth.

2. *Party Hats* Use Styrofoam cups, paper plates, food trays, crepe paper, feathers, ribbon, and other suitable items. Give each student identical materials. Have one student instruct the others how to construct the hat.

3. *Jewelry* Use different shapes of macaroni, straws cut into small pieces, string or shoelaces, and colored construction paper cut into different shapes with a hole punched in the middle. Give each student identical materials. Ask one student to tell the others how to make a necklace. Compare necklaces for accuracy. Then, put all materials back into the central area for the next student to make a necklace.

References

Ausberger, C. and Mullica, K. *How to Use Reproducible Illustrations in Language Remediation.* Syndatics, 1983.

Lloyd, P. and Beveridge, M. *Information and Meaning in Child Communication.* London: Academic Press, 1981.

Lucas, Ellyn. *Semantic and Pragmatic Language Disorders.* Aspen Systems Corp., 1980.

Staab, Clair. "Language Functions Elicited by Meaningful Activities: A New Dimension in Language Programs," *Language, Speech, and Hearing Services in Schools.* Volume 14, Number 3, July 1983.